resistance resistance resistance resistance
tance resistance resistance resistance resis
sistance resistance resistance resistance re
ce resistance resistance resistance resistan
tance resistance resistance resistance resis
sistance resistance resistance resistance re
ce resistance resistance resistance resistan
tance resistance resistance resistance resis
sistance resistance resistance resistance re
ce resistance resistance resistance resistan
tance resistance resistance resistance resis
sistance resistance resistance resistance re
ce resistance resistance resistance resistan
tance resistance resistance resistance resis
sistance resistance resistance resistance re
ce resistance resistance resistance resistan
tance resistance resistance resistance resis
sistance resistance resistance resistance re
ce resistance resistance resistance resistan
tance resistance resistance resistance resis
sistance resistance resistance **persist** resis
sistance resistance resistance resistance re
ce resistance resistance resistance resistan
tance resistance resistance resistance resis
sistance resistance resistance resistance re
ce resistance resistance resistance resistan
tance resistance resistance resistance resis
sistance resistance resistance resistance re
ce resistance resistance resistance resistan
tance resistance resistance resistance resis

Don't Give Up Just Yet

Don't Give Up

Choosing Persistence
in a World of
Overwhelming
Resistance

TYNDALE
MOMENTUM®

A Tyndale nonfiction imprint

Written by Nick Connolly

Foreword by Jess Connolly

Just Yet

Visit Tyndale online at tyndale.com.

Visit the author online at nickconnolly.com.

For information about special discounts for bulk purchases, please contact Tyndale House Publishers at csresponse@tyndale.com, or call 1-855-277-9400.

Library of Congress Cataloging-in-Publication Data

A catalog record for this book is available from the Library of Congress.

ISBN 978-1-4964-7836-8

Printed in China

30	29	28	27	26	25	24
7	6	5	4	3	2	1

To Jess, Elias, Glory, Benja, and Cannon.
I am the most blessed because of you all.

Contents

Foreword

Our family loves a little healthy competition.

A game of Monopoly, a challenge to see who can hold the longest plank, or even just a sloppy game of soccer—when none of us actually knows how to play.

One time, when we were waiting in line at a theme park, we all competed to see who could stand on one foot the longest.

We're all *just* stubborn enough to believe that we can outlast each other, and no matter how many times we lose, we sign up for each contest with determination and hope.

By now we should all know, however, that Nick is probably going to win.

He is definitely going to win Monopoly, and he for sure won that one-footed standing competition, but it's not because of force or bravado. He won't even brag when it's done. He has always had the gift of persistence, patience, and the vision that helps you hold on when it doesn't even make sense.

With almost twenty years of marriage and parenting under our belt, I've learned to let him cheer me on rather than competing against him. I've learned that if I can let his gentle wisdom and passionate coaching reframe my thoughts of defeat, I've got a solid chance to outlast whatever is coming against me.

Of course, now I'm talking less about a plank challenge and more about the callings that make up our lives. One of God's greatest gifts to me is pairing with me a pastor, a friend, and a husband (all in one human!) who is not only willing but able to help me push past the inevitable resistance and see what God has in store for me.

I grieve for Nick that he married a woman who could have been voted "Most Likely to Quit When It Gets Difficult," but I rejoice for you and me that he has written this book to give us the insight we desperately need in this season and the ones to come.

These words are going to help you.

These words will leave you feeling seen and met, unashamed about the resistance that surrounds you and equipped to press through it.

These words will leave you feeling more alert to your own desires, more able to fight your own defeat, and more awake to the callings that you're not meant to give up on, just yet.

More than anything, these words will leave you more connected to Jesus—the author and perfecter of your faith.

Take a deep breath. You're in the right spot.

Jess Connolly

I want to make sure you reap the harvest he has for you on the other side of the hard things you're currently facing.

Introduction

"I give up."

My wife, Jess, and I were in the kitchen on a Saturday morning. The kids were buzzing around us as they made breakfast. One was making oatmeal, another was spreading way too much Nutella on a piece of toast, and cereal boxes were all over the counter. I had just spent time reading my Bible and simply being still. But even though I had just refueled my heart, rather than looking forward to Sunday, I was trying to figure out how I could avoid it.

Not a great state of mind for a pastor.

Our kitchen had the same energy as a Waffle House late on a Saturday night which, if you don't know the reference, is a *lot* of energy. But I was struggling. Discouraged. Jess could tell, and she sat down beside me at the table. Touched my shoulder.

Those three words left my mouth as a breath—I was too exhausted and defeated to use my voice, to even give a firm two-weeks' notice. If I didn't have enough energy to enunciate my plans, I certainly didn't have the energy to officially type up my resignation, hand it in, and formally walk away from the thing I had once felt so sure I was called to do.

You wouldn't have guessed it from the outside. To an observer, I looked like a happy guy standing with his beautiful wife in the kitchen of their brand-new home in a fantastic city. Our four incredible children were creating chaos around us as we talked: we had officially entered into a new season of independence where they prepared their *own* breakfasts. This was a new level of parental freedom.

But I couldn't even muster a smile. Instead, all I could think about was leaving my job—walking away from the dream I had poured my life into building. Things were hard. People were hard. I'm sure I was difficult at times. I know, pastors are supposed to carry a cheerful spirit of optimism like Ted Lasso, with the vigor of an Olympic athlete, topped off with a little bit of Fortune 500 CEO. *Sometimes* I'm like that—I'm a dreamer, after all—but if I'm honest, I hadn't felt that way in a long time.

I was done.

This was a no-gas-left-in-the-tank resignation.

I had no more strength for sermon prep and staff meetings. No vision for the areas where our church could grow. No willingness to meet another person for counseling over coffee. I couldn't even find the energy to refill my heart with what would refresh me. My time in the Scripture had become dry. My prayers seemed to be received by a void, rather than by God. The things that of old had replenished—now felt ineffective.

Worst of all, I had no more energy to love my wife like I wanted to. I was too tired even to take my kids on fun adventures. Honestly, I had no motivation for anything.

That moment in the kitchen with Jess wasn't the result of a tough week or even a series of tough weeks. It wasn't just a difficult season—as we like to say in the church. These were years of pain, exhaustion, and even despair. Later in this book I'll get into what made those years so hard, but for now, just know that if you find yourself in a similar moment, you are not alone. I see you, and I hear you. I've been there.

I've had my pain, and you've had yours. We each have had our unique struggles. The important thread we share is that we all face resistance. By *resistance*, I mean anything that's causing discouragement, defeat, or even despair in your life. A sense of pushback making every day seem to be an uphill climb rather than a gentle coast. And the pain from that resistance hurts a lot.

Maybe it's a dream that hasn't quite worked out like you'd hoped.

It could be a marriage that's past the days of "for better" and has entered into a time of "for worse." You wonder if staying isn't worth the fight anymore—and the future of your family is on the line.

Maybe a friendship or another key relationship has gone awry. You can't imagine your life without this person, but right now, you can't take another day *with* them, either.

Maybe it's a lack of connection that has you ready to call it quits. After finding yourself in the deep end of a desire to date and hopefully marry one day, dead end after dead end of endless swiping has convinced you to consider a monastic lifestyle.

Relocations and job switches always promise a big payoff. Who doesn't love a new start, especially when the old way is filled

We all face resistance.

I see you, and I hear you. I've been there.

with so much pain? But once the newness wears off and the challenges arise, will giving up and trying somewhere new be your go-to option *again*?

The list only gets longer. It may seem like whatever you attempt, there's an overwhelming sense of persistent resistance clouding your life.

If you have ever felt hard-pressed, fed up, and ready to quit—my hope is, this book will be your companion. A source of gentle guidance about what to expect and encouragement to access a place of greater persistence and deeper strength—because I know it's in you.

If you follow Jesus, avoiding hard times and escaping pain is impossible. Jesus warned his friends that life would not be easy, telling them, "In this world you will have trouble" (John 16:33). There's zero equivocation in that.

But look at what he says next: "Take heart! I have overcome the world."

And on those days when we feel like we really just want to quit— whether it's our calling, our faith, our family, or the cornerstone rhythms of life that keep us healthy and whole—on those days, we need a good path forward, and we need something at the ready that's going to help us hang on just a little longer. Because it's right there in the verse: Jesus has overcome all the trouble this world can throw at us. There *is* a harvest on the other side of hard trials. Right now, handing in your two-weeks' notice feels like all the harvest you need, and I get that.

But what if there's more?

Jesus has overcome all the trouble this world can throw at us.

The Scriptures speak of a harvest for those who are willing to persevere through the hard things in life. I want to make sure you reap the harvest he has for you on the other side of the hard things you're currently facing.

Because hard things are always going to come. I'm sorry to say, but my words aren't going to make all your problems go away. The instinct you have to quit—to walk away while it all burns down—isn't going to go anywhere. But if we can befriend that resistance we're facing—if we can learn to acknowledge it, understand it, and be honest with God about it—we will become better equipped to make our way through it.

With that in mind, we're going to get real in this book. We'll dig deep into what the Scriptures have to say about hardship and persistence through it, about what we can learn from these dark nights of the soul. We'll take a look at seven different areas of our lives where resistance seems to continually pop up and wreak havoc. And in the final part, we'll learn how—with God's help—we can hang on to him in each of these areas so that we can walk more confidently in who he made us to be—and emerge in the victory he has won for us.

But let's not get ahead of ourselves. "Just one more page" is the name of the game as we take this journey together. I believe, if you'll take it page by page, we'll get through the dark days together. I don't say that lightly. I speak as one who almost walked away from something very dear to me. In these pages I'll show you what encouraged me to persevere. To stay persistent through the resistance. And I hope it will encourage you too.

We'll get through the dark days together.

Here's what I wish I could go back and tell that guy in the kitchen.

Here's what I believe Jesus would say to him.

Here's what I want to say to you today.

Don't give up. Not just yet.

Now, in the pages to come, let's find out why.

Part I

Befriending Resistance

What if I told you there's more to your situation than meets the eye?

What if I told you that you aren't alone? That the "raining and pouring" feeling is a part of being the people of God?

What if I told you that resistance isn't merely a foe but can also be a friend?

A Time to Quit

Sometimes parting ways ensures persistence.

I love the show *Ted Lasso*.

In fact, I'll go on the record and say it's one of my favorite shows ever. For me it's the right amount of humor, sports, and the human heart—all while making witty cultural references. Not to mention it's based in the UK, and one of my most favorite cities is London. It's an incredible cocktail of all my favorite likes.

Don't worry, I won't give away too much, but one of the dynamics of the show is Ted coming to grips with the idea of quitting. Ted, being a coach and natural encourager, always desires for people to keep going and finish the task, match, or whatever they're doing in life.

Quitting isn't an option for Ted.

> **We have to acknowledge the elephant in the room: sometimes walking away is the right choice.**

As we find out, this is a pretty deeply rooted idea. We learn his father took his own life—and because of this trauma, Ted feels like his father "quit" on him. This revelation is a powerful moment for the viewer—but it also captures some of the tension you might be feeling as you begin to read this book.

When we encounter resistance, how do we know when to keep going? And how do we know when it's okay to walk away? As the theologian Kenny Rogers once sang,

> *You've got to know when to hold 'em*
> *Know when to fold 'em*
> *Know when to walk away*[1]

Surely we can't continue to do everything, always and forever.

Here's one thing I've noticed about our culture—we don't do tension very well. We favor black and white over gray. We value a quick Google search for the answer over meaningful discovery that takes time. Quick. Now. Hurry. Yes. No. These describe our typical default.

This book is about persistence, especially in the face of resistance, but before we discuss how to do that, we have to acknowledge the elephant in the room: sometimes walking away is the right choice. Sometimes parting ways ensures persistence. But ultimately, there's a tension here we must learn to embrace: persistence is not black and white. There are times to push through, to keep going. But *there will also be times when quitting and stepping away from a situation is not only necessary but imperative.* Sometimes giving up on something in your life will actually *ensure* that you'll persist—not in that situation, but in your life.

Let me give you some examples of times when walking away is the right decision.

WHEN THE SITUATION IS TOXIC

A few years into marriage, Jess and I sensed the need to make a very difficult decision. The details themselves don't matter: we knew we needed to be obedient to God and trust him with the consequences of our decision.[2]

And we knew this decision would affect not only us, but also those closest to us. Nonetheless, we made the decision as a married couple and made the decision known to family. Immediately we received backlash and anger. This response seemed to dominate every conversation I would have with that side of our family. Despite multiple attempts to lovingly change the subject and move on, it became clear things weren't getting better. They were actually getting worse. Then "worse" ended up moving into toxic speech toward our family and me. The hurtful accusations became less about our decision and became really personal.

After much prayer, I knew it was time to offer up an ultimatum: we needed this relationship to move in a healthy direction or it was time to move on. Unfortunately (and painfully), it ended up being the latter. We put a pause on the relationship until we could see fruitful change or come to a point of reconciliation. We made it very clear this wasn't goodbye forever, it was merely goodbye until things changed.

Oftentimes I find myself reciting this phrase: "Even Jesus disappointed people, and he was perfect!" Even though

Sometimes giving up on something in your life will actually *ensure* that you'll persist—not in that situation, but in your life.

disappointing people is a part of life, it's still difficult. And if you add family dynamics, it makes it near impossible.

At some point in your life, I know you will face a similar situation. The toxic words may come not from a family member but from a different relationship in your life. It might not be a toxic relationship at all, but rather a toxic working or living environment.

Let me be very clear: in order to persevere healthfully in life, sometimes a pause will be required. It might be for good. It might be temporary. Again, there's that dreaded tension rearing its head.

I can't tell you what the right decision is. But I do know that God will guide.

WHEN THE SITUATION IS HARMFUL

It must be said that sometimes situations aren't merely toxic, but in fact are actually harmful to us. Abuse—whether physical, sexual, or emotional—should not be tolerated or endured in the name of persistence.

There are many people out there who will try to convince you otherwise; they'll guilt you into staying in a relationship that is harmful. Unfortunately, they might even offer gospel truths to support their guilt arguments.

Let me be clear: this is far from the heart of the gospel—and the Father. Should you find yourself in harmful circumstances, seek counsel and professional help to the best of your ability. I have witnessed firsthand how a brave individual can be rewarded with breakthrough when they seek help.

Bottom line, we must never confuse persistence with permitting abuse.

RIGHT SITUATION, WRONG TIME

Finally, there are instances when it's just not God's timing or plan. It takes discernment to know when to persevere and when to wait or even pivot completely.

I learned this during my wife's and my journey to found our church, Bright City. I hope to tell you more about this wonderful community we're a part of throughout our time together, but for now here's something most people don't know: even though our church was established in 2014, we actually tried to begin it much earlier—actually six years earlier.

Our family had just come out of a hard time, but we were still hanging on to our dream of believing God would give us the chance to birth something very dear to our hearts, a community church. Despite feeling discouraged from difficulties in a previous church community, three times we sought to raise funds and begin the process. And three times we sensed a little resistance in the form of logistical and financial roadblocks.

We were faced with a decision: We could quit and walk away, forgetting the dream. We could keep going, trying to knock down the door and start our church regardless of the resistance in our path. Or a third option—we could pause in order to gain some perspective. After much prayer and waiting, we embraced what God seemed to be showing us—to wait.

In retrospect, if we had continued, it would have most definitely cost us our spiritual health and vitality. We would've ultimately ended up hating God, each other, and the church. Additionally, we would've replicated that unhealth in other people. Bottom line, it was the wrong time for the right thing. And the right thing at the wrong time usually makes for the wrong outcome.

Have you ever had something like this happen in your life? Maybe you find yourself there now. You're on the cusp of making a critical move, but you're more unsettled than peaceful. To make the thing happen now could cost your health. Or even worse, fracture your relationship with God.

The thing is, God's plan for our lives is not that we just "do the thing" for the sake of doing it. He wants us to experience abundance. If "doing the thing" comes at the cost of abundance, it might actually be time to pause or even walk away. A mutual, loving relationship with God is always the goal.

Here's what I found out through our season of waiting. For one, it wasn't merely a pause but a time of necessary preparation. We tend to think a "no" or "not now" means we're standing still or moving two steps back. That's not the case with God. He works in our life when our life calls for a momentary break.

Another piece of wisdom surfaced out of the pause. I learned that God knew me better than I knew myself. You're probably wondering what the deferred dream was. The deep desire was to birth a new faith community in Boston, Massachusetts. We established relationships, took many trips to familiarize ourselves with the area, and even got Boston area codes for our mobile phone numbers. Turns out, I'm made more for the southeast than the northeast. It took a little bit of humbling to see this. Could I have started? Absolutely. Would I have

> We tend to think a "no" or "not now" means we're standing still or moving two steps back. That's not the case with God.

> **Cost and surrender should lead us to love God more, not hate him.**

finished? I don't think so. God knew that then, and I know that now. He knows you better than you do. Rather than kicking against the goads (see Acts 26:14), pause to let God work out the details. He knows you perfectly and intimately.

There should be no pride in your heart if you need to pivot in life or shame if that's what you decide to do. People pivot all the time. Perseverance requires a course correction every once in a while. Does following Jesus come at a cost and require absolute surrender? Absolutely. But cost and surrender should lead us to love God more, not hate him. God doesn't need a circumstantial martyr—someone who sticks it out just so you can say you didn't give up. He already has the perfect martyr. His name is Jesus. No, God's desire for you and me is to follow him in surrender and obedience so we may flourish and grow. Don't stunt your spiritual growth through prideful persistence.

If you're in a situation like ours, try asking the question, "Would continuing in this cause me to love or hate God more?" Be careful, however, with this answer. Sometimes blessing and comfort squelch our love for God too.

The answer will guide you to your next move.

THE ONE PERCENT

I know it may seem counterintuitive, starting a book on persistence with talking about when you *shouldn't* persist. But the thing is, I need you to start this book knowing that the kind of persistence I'm talking about is not one-size-fits-all. It's not a nice, catchy phrase you could buy on a sign at Hobby Lobby and hang in your kitchen. The presence of resistance always, *always* requires discernment. And discernment is always needed in the tension—the middle. I know God will guide and give you direction.

There's an exception to every rule. This is the one percent. Pausing. Pivoting. Graciously and gracefully giving up. Now let's look at the 99 percent: the times when life does call for persistence in the midst of resistance. And let's learn how we can flourish by committing to continuing instead of giving up.

2 Embracing Storms

We're not surprised by the storms, and we aren't surprised by the calm. We expect both.

My family and I have been fortunate to live in many different areas of the United States. One thing we've learned is that no matter where you live, there will be trade-offs. Particularly when it comes to weather.

When we lived in the beautiful Pacific Northwest, we experienced two extremely beautiful months per year. The shades of green, the sunshine, the perfect temperatures, the crystal-clear waters, the contrast of the mountains against the sky—the place was stunning. Those two months, however, were sandwiched in between ten of the rainiest months. It was almost as if a faucet from the heavenlies was constantly leaking.

> I was *offended* by resistance. How dare it creep into my life at all, much less uninvited?

We spent some time in the Midwest as well, where colors present themselves in fall unlike any other place I've ever lived. From the sky to the trees, there are burning oranges and bright reds. One can only experience and never explain what it's like. But then there's the snow. The Connollys are made for a lot of things, but snow isn't one of them. The last few months we were living there we experienced "Mother's Day snow." And it wasn't just a dusting to remind us winter still exists. It was almost two feet. We left Indiana the first week of June.

Now the Low Country of South Carolina is where we call home. There's magic here too . . . if you look past the horrid humidity. The colors of green that present themselves off of the marsh during a sunset or a sunrise are breathtaking. And then there's the beach. The salt. The sand. The water. The temperature can be cold, mild, or warm—it doesn't matter. Moments spent at the beach always restore my soul.

The trade-off, you ask?

We get hurricanes. Tropical storms. Depressions. Categories 1 through 3 and sometimes 4 and 5.

The thing is, because we live here, we aren't surprised by the storms. In fact, we *expect* some sort of storm warning every year. Hurricane season has its window—and so we know how to be prepared and make arrangements at a moment's notice. This year we experienced a Category 1 that slightly peeled back the overhang of our roof and clipped the top of a large tree in our backyard. It took out a fence we shared with our neighbor. The trade-off felt a little harder this year.

We're not surprised by the storms, and we aren't surprised by the calm. We expect both.

OFFENDED BY RESISTANCE

I wish I could say this was true for my spiritual life.

A few years ago, I noticed something about my outlook on life: I found myself surprised by the pain and hurt from life's storms. If a relationship became hard, I was shocked. If a conflict arose at the church, I couldn't believe it. If money was tight, I was stunned by the audacity of God.

Maybe *surprised* isn't the word. I was *offended* by resistance. How dare it creep into my life at all, much less uninvited?

"Why is this so hard?"

"Where's the momentum?"

"Could this job *be* any more boring?"

I'm not proud to say this, but I genuinely believed a good life lived meant only "good weather" experienced. As I scrolled social media, throwing myself into the deep end of comparison, I thought prosperity and pain-free living was par for the course. If I just did the right thing and acted the right way, I could avoid any pain or resistance that might arise.

It didn't work.

Not only did it not work, it actually made things worse. I became angry and bitter. Finally, I came to God with an ultimatum: "Stop these storms—or else!" Have you ever prayed something like

Eventually I realized the truth: I could continue to be surprised and offended by the presence of storms in my life—or I could embrace them.

that? (I didn't really have an "or else"; it just felt right in the moment.)

Ultimatums aren't good in any relationship, but they are especially bad in a relationship with God. (It's not that God can't take my anger and bitterness—in fact, he's the only one who can and will. It's just not the best way to experience the loving abundance promised by God.) And again, my demands didn't help my situation—they didn't make the hard times go away.

Eventually I realized the truth: I could continue to be surprised and offended by the presence of storms in my life—or I could embrace them.

Maybe you're like me. Do you find yourself surprised—even shocked by life's storms? Have you, too, grown bitter or angry at God due to the pain of your problems? Has your consistent experience of resistance caused unwanted reactions in your heart and soul toward life, others, and maybe even God himself?

What if we *expected* resistance, instead of being continually surprised by it? What if, like the sage Carolinians, we were prepared for storms and knew how to make arrangements at a moment's notice?

Weathering the storms in life is never easy, but a shift in our perspective can help us stand firm—especially in life's toughest moments of resistance.

REFRAME AND REMAIN

When I first got serious about Bible reading in high school, I immediately flipped open to the book of James. Why? I was young and probably prideful (you can take *probably* out of that sentence), I had heard it was one of the harder books of the Bible, and I liked the idea of a challenge. And in my pride, I took it even further: I wasn't going to just *read* the book of James, I was going to *memorize* the book of James.

Well, the hard part about me memorizing the book of James is that I didn't memorize the book of James.

But here's the beautiful part about me memorizing James: I did memorize the first four verses of chapter 1. (Can I get an amen if that's your story? Verses 1-4. That's all I did.)

Even in my failure, God was gracious. Those few verses would guide me through the fifteen hardest years of my life. It was a time filled with wave after wave of resistance: crushed dreams, loss of loved ones, extreme poverty, toxic communities, medical crises. These verses were my constant companion:

> *Consider it pure joy, my brothers and sisters, whenever you face trials of many kinds, because you know that the testing of your faith produces perseverance. Let perseverance finish its work so that you may be mature and complete, not lacking anything.*
> JAMES 1:2-4

I've been spending time in James again lately (still not memorized). It can be easy to misunderstand James's intent here in these verses, especially in that opening where he encourages us to consider trials pure joy. It might feel like he's asking us to fake it till we make it. *Oh, everything's great, just another flat tire. I consider this pure joy!*

False joy produces a false (or inauthentic) relationship with God. James doesn't want us to fake it. This world does a great job trying to convince us that joy is circumstantial. I think he's wanting us to see God is working in times of testing, and that should bring us joy.

Recently I've noticed two encouragements in the passage I hadn't noticed before.

Reframe the Lies

James's first encouragement is to *reframe* the lies we are believing about resistance. And the first lie we often believe is that we're somehow at fault, that we've brought the resistance upon ourselves, that resistance is the result of *something we've done*. Actually, there's something greater going on here: resistance is actually a result of *who we are*. Let me explain.

You are family. A child of God. And the hard part about being in the family of God is that Satan has a target on your back. He is going to do everything in his power to keep you from walking in the fullness of being God's child. He's going to whisper lies in the midst of life's storms, that your pain means that God is somehow displeased with you, or that you've done something wrong to deserve this.

My brothers and sisters, nothing could be further from the truth.

The truth—the key to weathering persistent resistance—is actually in the phrase "my brothers and sisters." James reminds us that we are first and foremost children of God. It's the core of who we are, the most important part of our identity.

When resistance is persistent, it's because the enemy *knows* you're a child of God. It's because he *knows* God has a plan and a

When resistance is persistent, it's because the enemy *knows* you're a child of God.

purpose for your life. Now, like me, you're probably wondering how we can know which trials are from Satan—and I don't have the answer for you. We'll come back to this later. Here's what I do know: Satan might not be the cause of every trial, but he will certainly seek to capitalize on anything and everything he can so you will forget who you are and give up and walk away from a life with Christ.

So this is the first reframe we must keep at the center of our attention: when we face persistent resistance, it's a reminder that we're children of God, that he *chose* us.

And it also means he's up to something in our lives.

There's a second lie that the enemy whispers to us in the midst of trials: that our pain means we're heading in the wrong direction, away from God's calling. But I soon noticed that if I was trying to walk in a good and godly way, my life was actually harder.

If I vowed to love a difficult person, they became more difficult.

If I wanted to commit to early morning sessions studying Scripture and spending more time with God, I was overcome with exhaustion and the need for more sleep.

If I wanted to obey him, temptation and distraction seemed to increase tenfold.

The fact is, every good and worthwhile endeavor is met with resistance—because the enemy doesn't want you to have God's best in your life. He doesn't want you to have a good marriage. He doesn't want you to have good and meaningful relationships. He doesn't want you to be generous with your time and gifts. He wants you to live in fear instead of stepping into your God-given purpose. Most importantly, he doesn't want you to grow or reach the maturity James promises is the result of persistence. Maturity is the right way, and resistance is one of his weapons.

What is the hard thing that you're doing right now? Maybe that's *the* thing you're supposed to be doing in your life. Rather than thinking you've gone the wrong way, let's reframe: Can you ask God if the resistance is because it's affirmation of the *right way*?

I know it's hard. But if we can reframe our circumstance in this way, then we *can* consider our trials pure joy, as James says we should. If we can remember the truth of who we are and our purpose in this life—that will be enough to keep our heads in the game. Resistance is persistent, but you know what? So is God. And because he lives in you—so are you.

Remain in Him

Once we can reframe the resistance we are experiencing through the lens of our God-given identity, these first verses in James offer another encouragement: to *remain*.

It's hard to stick with things if we don't find them productive or efficient. But persistent resistance actually *is* productive. It's not meaningless. There's a process that's happening through these experiences, and it's preparing us for what God has for us in the future, making us a more complete person. It's producing a persistence inside us, a lasting work in our hearts to help us outlast the resistance of life. We are to "let perseverance finish its work," as James reminds us. From personal experience I've noticed that resisting the work God's doing in us produces an unhealthy soul.

> Resistance is persistent, but you know what? So is God. And because he lives in you— so are you.

> **We get in the way of his work if we give up every time things get tough.**

Have you ever noticed that even though you might change a relationship, or the place you live, or even the place you worship, when you find the new one, the same issues and pain points meet you there? This is very evident in my own life. In my early twenties, my answer to workplace drama was to get another job. But you guessed it, even though I changed locations, the drama didn't change. In fact, I noticed the pattern—it was me. Ouch.

At the end of the day, the solution isn't found in a physical move but in allowing God to finish his spiritual work in our hearts and souls. We get in the way of his work if we give up every time things get tough.

It can be easy to believe that we will develop into the people God wants us to be through new rhythms, how-tos, podcasts, and adventures—but in reality, it is staying consistent that allows God's work to be complete. There's power in staying—in remaining.

PERSISTENCE IS WHO YOU ARE

Recently my wife and I found ourselves in the midst of some stormy resistance. It was close to home, and it hurt deeply. Additionally I had no control in the matter. We were at the mercy of the winds and rain.

But even though there was initial pain and weariness, this time wasn't like the past, by the grace of God. I reacted differently. I didn't rail against God or daydream about packing up and moving on to a different circumstance. We withstood the initial blows with truths about who God is. About who we are—children of the Most High. The resistance was all the proof we needed. We sought God, and he confirmed that, even though the path was so painful, we were heading in the right direction. We resolved to remain steadfast and persistent in the midst of the resistance, believing that God was and is doing something in our lives, even if we can't see it.

We aren't ready to give up just yet.

My prayer is that this will be true for you too. No matter what storms may come, you'll grow less shocked and surprised. You'll learn to prepare and expect them, and you'll allow them to confirm what you know deep down—that you're a child of God. I pray that the resistance will become the comforting confirmation you need to know you're heading in the right direction.

The enemy hates when we reframe and remain—but that's his problem. God's people are a people of persistence. You are going to be persistent in the midst of resistance because that is who you are. If you have Christ in you, then that's who you are.

So keep going. One more step. One more page.

3

Surrounded by a Cloud

Whether you're in trial or tribulation, if you feel the urge to give up on God or on what he's given you—you're in good company.

Here's God's honest truth—you aren't the only one who's looked giving up straight in the face.

It doesn't always feel that way, does it? There's one feeling that frequently overwhelms me when I'm in the thick of trial: a sense of being alone. *I'm the only one who's ever faced a challenge like this. No one understands*, I think.

If the circumstances themselves don't push you to believe this, the push notifications from your go-to social media sure will. Why does it feel like everyone I follow has days filled with travel, amazing food, and an entourage of friends? Good vibes only—as the kids say.

As we saw in the previous chapter, Satan seeks to steal, kill, and destroy—and he does so in times of challenge by planting

You aren't the only one who's looked giving up straight in the face.

lies in our hearts about who we are and what God has called us to do, telling us that pain means that God doesn't like us or that we're heading in the wrong direction.

But the other tactic he uses? Isolation.

It's not enough to expect the storms of life. It's not enough to whisper pithy statements like "when it rains, it pours" as life downpours torrentially. If only it were that easy. When we feel like we are the only ones who have ever experienced this level of resistance, we need a faith system that will help us fight back. No, encourage us to fight back. We need stories of men and women who encountered resistance with faithfulness—and honestly, even temporary faithlessness—if we're to develop a persistent spirit.

And the Bible is *filled* with these stories. It feels like on every page, there's someone on the brink of giving up. This isn't some ploy to catch you up on your yearly Bible reading plan. If we are going to persist through resistance, we have to fight the lie that we are the only one. We need to consider stories of faithful (or failing!) men and women so that we can root ourselves in the fact that what we're experiencing is *absolutely normal*. And *even though it might not feel like it*, God is with us at every moment.

There's so much we can learn from studying resistance and persistence in the Bible. The goal of our time right now is to illuminate what some might know to be true—or want to believe is true—through the lens of persistence. As one desperate father in Scripture said, "I want to believe; help my unbelief" (see Mark 9:24).

And if that's you, that's more than fine.

Let's get going. We've got a lot of ground to cover.

RESISTANCE IN PARADISE

Resistance started in the Garden.

Eden was perfection. Adam and Eve experienced marital harmony. (Who knew it actually was possible?!) The days ranged from pleasantly cool in the morning to blissfully warm by the afternoon. (I'm talking the good kind of warm. As one who makes his home in the Southeast, the absence of humidity is a big deal to me.)

Not only was the temperature perfect but the setting was too. The untouched beauty of creation was everywhere. It was lush. Green. Colorful. Bountiful. Wild even. We are told fruit was within reach at all times. The rivers were clean and perfectly flowing— water levels not too high nor too low.

Many have pictured Eden as a permanent vacation. I know I used to. But a closer read showed me I was mistaken. There was actually responsibility and work—minus the complicated commute and the normal office boredom. But here's the beautiful part: work was meaningful and free from toil. Accomplishing "flow state" wasn't fleeting, and there was no micromanaging. If you do beautiful work by managing your home and caring for your children, picture it like this: instead of tiny tyrants trying to boss you around, your kids are consistently obedient and helpful. God commissioned Adam and Eve to rule over creation, and he gave them authority to make decisions and carry them out when desired.

Additionally, Eden was a foodie's paradise. You wouldn't have needed a Yelp review to know it was good. I imagine finding some of my favorite produce ripe whenever I wanted it.

It really was a perfect playground—created for the created by the perfect Creator himself. But I haven't even mentioned the best part yet. God walked among them and spoke freely to them. Imagine that! The presence of God within reach at all times. Never would they have said, "I just feel distant from God right now." It wasn't possible.

But even there where the grass was green—greener than the greens of Augusta National—the temptation to give up was right there in their midst.

The pressure to give up is present in blessing too.

Even in perfection, choosing persistence over giving up can be a struggle. I find this oddly encouraging. Often I buy the lie that if the resistance were nonexistent, so would be the temptation to give up. But that just isn't it. In lack and in plenty, in abundance and scarcity, the siren of our souls tempting us to type out our two-weeks' notice is always nearby.

In fact, I would argue that sometimes the voice telling me to give up booms louder in blessing. I don't want us to get ahead of ourselves in this biblical roundup, but I do need to make an important connection: the wheels consistently wobbled for Israel in times of blessing, not hardship. With a quick read of God's Word, one can see that blessing actually led them toward self-dependency and idolatry—which is another form of giving up.

Back to Adam and Eve. Life was good, but even there, the whispers of Satan embodying a serpent filled their ears—and hearts.

"This is nice, but wouldn't it be even better if you ate that other fruit? Why does God want to keep that from you?"

"Maybe you know better than God?"

"Didn't God give you all authority to make some life decisions on your own?"

They gave up and gave in. What exactly did Adam and Eve give up on? Belief and faith. Trust. God's word and promises for Satan's. The assignment given to them. Their responsibilities and work. Blessing. Each other—to name a few. Letting go can affect our legacy.

Giving up changed their lives and ours—forever.

GREAT PROMISES CAN'T BE PROBLEM-SOLVED

It almost seems like the bigger the promise, the greater the persistence needed.

Abram received a promise from God that would form a whole nation and people group—can you imagine receiving a promise like that? The promise would come through a child he and his wife desperately longed for. God first spoke to them in Genesis 12 by assuring Abram he'd be a father one day. What's the big deal, you ask?

Abram was seventy-five at the time.

You guessed it. He and God had a good laugh about the matter, and Abram continued on in life. But eventually he grew tired of waiting and gave up.

The bigger the promise, the greater the persistence needed.

Rather than being encouraged to persevere for the promise, Abram grew bitter and tired of waiting on God. He wasn't the only one. Sarai, his wife, was over the wait too. They took matters into their own hands. Their plan was for Abram to be unfaithful in his marriage with an employee of theirs. Eventually they got a child from this union (Ishmael), but it wasn't the *promised* child.

When we see the whole story written out in the Bible—when we can see that the blessing is indeed coming—this seems totally crazy. But man, I do the same thing. I turn a promise from God into a problem to be solved by me. Meaning it's up to me to cause the promise to be fulfilled by my might. I get tired of waiting for the blessing, assume God has forgotten the promise, or try to move up the timeline—I give up on God and take it on myself.

The good news is that even though Abram and Sarai had given up on God, even though they didn't persevere for the promise, God hadn't given up on them. The promise was still theirs for the receiving. When Abram (now called Abraham) was one hundred years old, he finally held the child of promise. His very own son.

The persistence needed for this promise took twenty-five years!

Here's what we need to learn: God isn't a microwave. God isn't an Instant Pot. God is like a Crock-Pot—slowly cooking the circumstances needed to eventually serve us the fulfillment of a promise. And his great promises require patient persistence.

WHEN THE SPIRITUAL HIGH WEARS OFF

I've become obsessed with all things "crown" involving the royal family. Naturally I was following all the events surrounding

God isn't a microwave. God isn't an Instant Pot. God is like a Crock-Pot—slowly cooking the circumstances needed to eventually serve us the fulfillment of a promise.

the transition of the throne from Queen Elizabeth II to King Charles III. Once the country grieved properly for the queen, the exciting details of the new king filled the air. There was an energy to it all. The king was on every TV station. He was being whisked away to this event and that appearance. The pace to it all was astounding.

King David from the Bible experienced the exact opposite. God's plan was for David to sit on the throne. The path toward the promise, however, would come through persistence. His anointing was followed by fifteen years of average. Once he had been anointed and made king of Israel, he went right back to working his day job. Instead of kingly prominence, he headed back to the pastures. I can't imagine what it would've been like to receive the promise of being king, only to barely persevere through the routine of everyday life. He should've been preparing his court and counsel; instead he was counting livestock. He should've been initiating policy. Instead he found himself trying to persist through mundane moments.

I used to feel so bummed when I sensed God was doing something in a very powerful way, only to have to stay put myself. I'd experience these awesome "spiritual highs"—only to get discouraged by a lull of uneventful days that followed. Every high was followed by a perceived low.

Big dreams seemed out of reach because of dreadful jobs.

I desired certain gifts and skills but was met by the reality that I wasn't quite where I wanted to be.

The honeymoon phase was followed by paying bills and daily chores.

What we learn from King David is that when it comes to persistence, we need to expect the natural to follow the supernatural.

He persevered and received his promise as king. Not only that, David has always impressed me as one of the few people in Scripture to develop healthy and lasting relationships. He had a whole crew of men whom he cared about and who cared about him. Not to mention his bond with Jonathan could possibly be the greatest bromance ever. Those relationships wouldn't have come to fruition without enduring through resistance.

If you've experienced God in a mighty way, only to be met with the humdrum tasks of today, don't be discouraged. Treasure the time with God and press on in the mundane and average. Surely fulfillment is on the other side of your follow-through.

DELAYED FULFILLMENT

If you track the life of Moses, all you see is persistent resistance. From birth Moses faced an uphill climb: he was born into a time in history where a pharaoh tried to eliminate a whole generation of Hebrew boys. Then he persevered through forty years of living away from home in the wilderness. Eventually he would be called by God to complete a promised task. He would help God rescue the nation of Israel from Egypt. But it wasn't quite the cakewalk one might have expected after the compelling calling he received.

First he ran into issues with the pharaoh of Egypt. God told Moses to go and ask for the people to be released, but nothing changed. Pharaoh's heart grew hard.

> Treasure the time with God and press on in the mundane and average.

God kept his promise after all, even if Moses didn't experience it in his lifetime.

Eventually Pharaoh did free the people, but their newfound freedom only resulted in new resistance. There was the physical resistance. How would they cross an impossible body of water? Then once they passed through the water, they encountered provisional resistance—no food or water.

They say the definition of insanity is doing the same thing over and over again—but expecting different results. But I call that walking with God. Sometimes the calling requires you and me to do the same thing over and over again and expect different results. That involves persistence. And Moses persisted.

You're probably thinking, *Nick, I know the story of Moses. Thank you,* Prince of Egypt. *He doesn't get to experience the promise on the other side of persistent resistance. See, Nick, sometimes persistence doesn't pay off.*

And by that you mean the Promised Land. Moses never got to set foot in the Promised Land.

Recently my wife and were talking with our dear friend Joel, who is incredibly gifted with all things Bible and theology. He pointed out to me that Moses did in fact set foot in the Promised Land, and he did it in incredible style . . . far better than it would have been with the whiney people he was leading at the time.

He set foot in the Promised Land with Jesus—when he and Elijah talked with the Savior on the Mount of Transfiguration (see Matthew 17:1-8). And he did so in glory.

God kept his promise after all, even if Moses didn't experience it in his lifetime. Even though he could only see a sliver of the story, Moses persisted—and his persistence paid off.

WAITING IS THE ONLY WAY

The pain you're experiencing in this season isn't isolated. As a son or daughter of Christ, you are a part of a great story of resistance and persistence; it's baked into your Christian DNA. The biblical examples I've given here? Not even close to exhaustive. The Israelites waited over a thousand years for a Messiah;[1] Anna the prophetess waited decades before her eyes saw her Savior. The letters to the early church are laced with encouragement to persist in the face of unfathomable challenge and adversity. Not to mention the resistance Jesus endured.

Everything you're feeling right now makes total sense. Whether you're in trial or tribulation, if you feel the urge to give up on God or on what he's given you—you're in good company. Don't buy the lie that the enemy is selling, that you're alone in your pain. It takes great courage to remain persistent in the midst of resistance.

You might feel alone, but you are not. A great crowd of witnesses has run the race before you and they are cheering you on (see Hebrews 11:1–12:1). The days might feel lackluster. But fulfilled promises are ahead. Your persistence will be paid in full—whether in this life or the next.

Part II

Outlasting the Onslaught

The resistance in this world is overwhelming.

Our next step? Outlast the onslaught. To do so, we've got to come face-to-face with it. Some of these struggles will be very familiar. Others might seem foreign. It's important to understand them all.

Our goal isn't to compare wounds but find a commonality in them. Your pain is your pain, and my pain is mine. Don't let yourself look to the left or right and miss the path to persistence right in front of your feet.

Here we go, together.

Because together is the only way we're going to get through.

4 Manna in the Cushions

When Doubt Comes Knocking

Whenever I've felt the temptation to give up and give in, it's usually because somewhere in my soul I'm battling the pain of unmet expectations.

Scripture tells of God communicating through a whisper. But doubt? Doubt seems to use a megaphone. It shouts things like these:

You must provide! God will never take care of you!

What makes you think God's going to come through this time? He always has to bail you out!

Doubt heckles us day after day after day. Opportunity knocks politely—but doubt presses its finger on the doorbell *and* pounds on the door at the same time. It won't stop ringing and pounding until you open the door and let it barge in. If you're a dreamer, doubt seeks to make you a cynic. If you're hopeful, doubt has the unusual skill of turning that hope into heaviness. If you find yourself finally walking toward your life's calling, doubt is there to trip you.

And once inside the house of your heart, doubt begins to make itself at home.

DEATH AND DOUBTING

In 2004, after a yearslong battle with cancer, my mom entered the hospital for what would be the last time. She was driving to work, and all of a sudden she had to pull over because she couldn't breathe. The fluid in her lungs had gotten to be too much because of the cancer in her body.

From that May until early June of that year, my mom deteriorated rapidly. I was in the midst of college, traveling an hour and a half to be at her bedside or to sit in the hospital waiting room, followed by an hour and a half drive back. And in those long car rides, I remember praying over and over again. If you've ever walked with a loved one through a terminal illness, I don't have to tell you what I prayed for. My greatest longing, my deepest desire, my *expectation*? Healing. Miraculous healing in this life from cancer.

I poured out my heart to God—and my mom passed away.

Healing on this side of heaven didn't happen.

Afterward, you'd think the pain from the loss of my mom would wound the most. But for me, it was the unmet expectation that hurt almost more. I had *told* God what I wanted. I had looked my dreams and desires straight in the face—and now I had to look at the fact that those dreams didn't come true.

Who *wouldn't* start to doubt God, who *wouldn't* want to give up in a moment like that?

You thought something was going to turn out one way, but it ended up going completely the other.

A "ring by spring" while in college didn't manifest quite like you'd hoped.

Your dream of 2.5 kids and a picket fence turned into waiting years for your first house or even one child—much less 2.5.

Your business endeavor turned into a failed nightmare.

Hurts from your new faith community left you struggling with extreme doubt.

Your expectations for your teenager seem to be dissolving before your eyes.

On their own, expectations aren't inherently bad. They're really just pointing to our honest longings, the deep desires that reside in our heart, soul, and mind. They're our picture of how life should go. So when life doesn't turn out like that picture, we have to sit and reconcile with reality—we have to face the fact that the world *doesn't* follow our lead. That is *always* a painful moment!

Whenever I've felt the temptation to give up and give in, it's usually because somewhere in my soul I'm battling the pain of unmet expectations. Out of all the pain we feel on this side of heaven, unmet expectations can bring some of the most extreme anguish. But the thing is, when we get too wrapped

Expectations point to our honest longings, the deep desires that reside in our heart, soul, and mind.

> **Unmet expectations will ultimately burn us, leading us to a life consumed by doubt.**

up in our expectations, we can find ourselves clinging to our own plans, rather than opening our hands to God's plan. We try to become godlike over our life rather than letting God be God.

Unmet expectations will ultimately burn us, leading us to a life consumed by doubt, a life feeling distant from the Father.

LIVING IN EXPECTANCY

The only way I know how to push past failed expectations is to fight them with expectancy. Where failed expectations crush us, expectancy will breathe new life and faith into our souls. Our action is the same—an outcry of our desires to God—but our mindset is different. A mindset of expectancy waits with anticipation for *his* outcome.

> Expectations say, "I need this to happen exactly like this, or I can't be happy."

> Expectancy says, "God will move and do as he wishes, and I can't wait to see what he does."

> Expectations say, "I can only trust God if he does what I want."

> Expectancy says, "I don't know how God will move, but I trust that he will."

Now, living in expectancy isn't going to necessarily make the outcome what we want. It's not going to take away the pain of losing your mom; it's not going to make it hurt less when your dreams don't pan out the way you want them to. I wish that were true, but it isn't.

What living with expectancy does is allow us to view those hard outcomes through the eyes of our loving Father. It allows us to cling to Scriptures like Genesis 50:20 and Romans 8:28, Scriptures that teach us how all the details of our lives are continually woven together for good. Every detail—and especially the difficult ones. The Father loves to hear what we long for— what we desire and hope for—even when the outcome isn't what we want. And just because we don't get what we want doesn't mean that what we wanted was bad or not of Christ. In fact, most of the time, we have longing and desire only because they're given to us by him. As I tell my church frequently, "God-inspired longings make for great leadings in our lives." Being honest with him is part of being close to him.

The key is that you commit—over and over again, every single day—to trust him with the process *and* the outcome.

LOOSE-CHANGE MANNA

At the end of 2007, our family set out on an incredible and insane adventure: we were going to leave our hometown of Charlotte, North Carolina, and move over 3,000 miles away to a small town just outside of Seattle, Washington. That was the incredible part.

The insane part involved *why* we moved 3,000 miles. We moved to be houseparents at a maternity home. "What's a maternity home?" you ask. Great question. A maternity home is where young pregnant moms who need a place to stay (for whatever reason) can live until they give birth to their babies. There was room for up to ten women, who could move in at any time without warning. We encouraged and helped them as they made the

The key is that you commit—over and over again, every single day—to trust him with the process *and* the outcome.

best decisions for their future. So there we were, with two small children, living in the same house as a lot of young, vulnerable pregnant women. (Did I mention Jess was pregnant too?) Can we say major adjustment?

The clincher of the situation was that our income was based on whether or not we could raise financial support. At first this was no big deal, but if you recall, in 2008 our country's economy fell apart. For the Connollys, bad became worse, and worse became a dumpster fire really quick. After a while it became quite clear we needed a different plan if we wanted to survive. I jumped back into working retail and construction—whatever I had to do to support my family. But no matter what we did, it just seemed like we never could make ends meet.

I don't know what "financial hardship" means to you. Maybe it's not having the new car you want or having to cut back on going out and buying coffees every day so that you can pay all your bills. Maybe it's the stress of not having a large amount of money in your savings account. For us, it was consistently needing to search our car and house for change so that we could buy groceries. Any coins would do—we didn't discriminate. Honestly, I would've tried to roll up Chuck E. Cheese coins (if we'd had any).

Milk, eggs, bread, and peanut butter seemed to stretch us the longest, so that's all we ate. And, of course, we needed baby supplies too.

I'm telling you, those days were dark. And they went on for a few years. But they weren't necessarily darkest for the reason you might expect (our cash flow or lack thereof). Don't get me wrong, that was bad. But even worse was the fact that we had some big dreams—for our family, for our ministry, for what we believed God had called us to do—and no matter what we did, it felt like we couldn't catch a break to make them happen.

I remember being so mad at God. Why couldn't God let us have a lot or even just a little more than we currently had so we could begin to gain some sort of financial independence? I was tired of gathering change. Didn't he call us there? What were we going to do? Why had we left relative prosperity in Charlotte and entered into financial chaos 3,000 miles away from home?! Those dark days could quickly turn into doubt-filled days.

The Scriptures tell us the people of Israel asked these same doubting questions when they left Egypt. God made a miraculous way for them to escape the slavery and bondage of 430 years and step into freedom as their own nation. Their freedom would involve not just a change of location, but a change of heart. They needed to learn to trust God as a provider each and every day.

One of the ways God provided was by sending them manna from heaven. If you don't know what manna was, you're in good company—I teach the Bible for a living, and even I'm not sure what it really was. The Bible says it was kind of like small flakes and tasted like honey. But God provided it as their daily bread. And since many of us love bread and so many of us love bread and can't have bread (my GF friends), I'm sure it was pretty magical and miraculous stuff that everyone could have. But there was one problem: using Tupperware was seen as a lack of trust. You couldn't store any of it for the future. The Israelites had to trust that this bread would be provided every day, completely out of nowhere. Fresh bread is far better, but stored bread has its temptations too.

For the Israelites, every day required faith and dependence on God's provision. And twice as much faith on the sixth day for the seventh. Kind of like finding coins deep in a car seat or couch.

Eventually Israel would show glimpses of trust and dependence in God as their provider. But times of doubt would remain their struggle as a people indefinitely.

I know the feeling. Everything in me wants to graduate from manna moments and move into plentiful moments. I want to stop searching for coins and instead feel them jingling abundantly in my pocket. When provision is thin, so is my persistence. Any time I don't have a lot, especially money, I tend to doubt the most.

But I think Jesus wants to show us something greater. He gives us just enough to know he's enough.

A DECLARATION AND A DECISION

As he did with the Israelites, God often uses what I want to be a once-in-a-while occurrence as a staple in my life—not because he's malicious, but so that I can regularly remember the truth that *he* is my provider. That every day is an invitation to exercise faith. The goal is to awaken to a life of dependence on God. The goal is to know who our source and provider is in every season and situation. The goal was never to be self-sustaining.

That's what faith ultimately is, isn't it? Trust. An anchoring in expectancy; a belief that, regardless of what circumstances look

> The goal is to awaken to a life of dependence on God.

> **Faith is both a declaration made once *and* a decision made daily.**

like to our earthly eyes, God *will* provide. Committing to that trust over and over again.

Faith is both a declaration made once *and* a decision made daily.

Do you find yourself at the end of your rope, short of what's needed to keep going? In the middle of a financial need, desperately digging for coins to carry on? Do you find yourself in deep pain, wanting to pack up and give in, because of unchecked (and unmet) expectations?

A financial shortfall is often what sends me into a tailspin of doubt, but your kryptonite might be different from mine. Yet, even if our struggles are different, we all need to recognize doubt before it sends us into a downward spiral of discouragement, despair, and even worse—defeat.

Paul, a church leader during the first century, used a phrase I never really understood until recently. He encouraged his people to "take captive every thought to make it obedient to Christ" (2 Corinthians 10:5). Here's what this means: not every thought should be allowed to run free. Just because I think something doesn't mean that thought is true. If every thought were true, we'd all be in trouble.

When you and I encounter thoughts that lead to doubt, especially when it comes to our relationship with God, we've got to do our very best to capture them by speaking truth in response. How do we do this? Here are three questions that can help us take our thoughts captive by turning them away from doubt and back toward God's truth.

The first question I ask is this: Is what I'm choosing to believe *distracting*? I usually am distracted in my most doubt-filled seasons. Any time I fail to focus on what's of first importance, my faith suffers. I become distracted by the to-dos, the worries, the burdens, the have-nots—and the list goes on and on. They all become the object of my focus, and these objects make incredible catalysts for doubt.

In a moment where Jesus sensed doubt and apprehension among his followers, he reminded them that when we "seek first the kingdom of God," all the other stuff will take care of itself (Matthew 6:33, ESV). I think Jesus was being modest, because what he really means is "I'll take care of the rest." Distractions breed doubt, but focus on the right things breeds faith.

Another helpful question I often ask is this: Is what I'm believing *isolating*? Here's why. Isolation is to doubt like oxygen to an open flame—highly dangerous. Doubt causes us to shrink back when it comes to human interaction. I wonder if this is why Satan waited to approach Eve alone in the Garden. The greater the isolation, the greater the potential for doubt to take root and spread.

Sometimes we need to get alone to collect our thoughts, to think, and to pray. But when we isolate ourselves from healthy community, our doubts can take us captive. The cycle goes like this: I feel guilty for doubting God again. Then shame slow-saunters into my heart as I believe this is who I am, a doubter. Then I cut myself off from people who could strengthen my faith with their support and prayers. And so the cycle continues.

I don't think it's an accident that the writer of Hebrews connects the community of faith with each individual person of faith. In chapter 11, we see a list of faithful believers. In chapter 12, the author underscores the importance of community and faith, calling the believers who have gone before us a "great cloud of witnesses." What he means is that they are testifying to us about God's faithfulness—and cheering us on in our own race. You see, there's a correlation between community and faith: a great community around us can lead to greater faith in us. Unfortunately the converse is true for doubt. No community, plenty of doubt.

Maybe this is why Satan loves a solo Christian?

The last question is a big one for me. Is what I'm believing *limiting*? As I hope you've gotten to know me, I'm sure you can pick up that I struggle a lot with doubt and discouragement. Ultimately it's because I struggle with limiting belief.

Jesus could usually tolerate most people. He ate with tax collectors and sinners. He traveled with a group of difficult disciples who gave him a run for his money. He even tolerated religious banter from time to time. One thing he struggled to tolerate—limiting belief. Or a lack of faith. In fact, one time he had to change locations from one town to the next because there was such a limiting belief among the people (see Mark 6:1-6). Vulnerably speaking, there have been days when I know Jesus has wanted to move on from my "town" based off of what's rolling around in my brain.

This might seem insensitive at first, but you have to understand, God went out of his way to communicate very clearly that "with God, all things are possible." From the birth of Jesus, to the ministry of Jesus, to the resurrection of Jesus, all things are possible with God (see Luke 1:37; Matthew 19:26; and John 21:14).

And if all things are possible, nothing can limit God. If this is true, why do I find myself in spirals of negative self-talk? Why do I think things won't work out for me? Why do I limit who I am and what he's called me to?

Since we're getting really vulnerable, I'll share this. I still struggle when people call me "pastor." In fact, I fought it for a long time. It's not because I'm trying to be above trend or go by some other cool title like "TED-talk speaker" or "sage guide"—I just struggled to believe that God could grow that gift in me.

As you can see, limiting belief doesn't just produce doubt, it produces insecurity that is contrary to our identity in Jesus.

I wish I could tell you, "If you follow these guidelines, doubt won't stand a chance." But there *will* be hard days beside hospital beds for all of us. There *will* be expectations we put on God that don't work out like we'd hoped. And for some of us, moments of relying on daily provision of manna await us in the future.

We won't be able to avoid doubt, but we can certainly resist it. May these stories remind you that you aren't alone, even though you feel like it. And may these questions help you capture the discouraging, doubtful thoughts and apply truth accordingly. If you do so, I know you will remain persistent in your fight against doubt.

> Limiting belief doesn't just produce doubt, it produces insecurity that is contrary to our identity in Jesus.

5

A Thousand Deaths

When Hardship Hits

The loss happened on a day, but I will feel it for a lifetime.

We can work through doubt. But hardship? Hardship hits differently.

I don't know what kind of hardship you've experienced, but I know for a fact that you have experienced some. Maybe it was the diagnosis of a debilitating disability or a long-term illness. Maybe it was the unexpected or expected loss of a loved one, or a job, or a dream. It could've been a huge breach of trust and/or covenant in marriage, or some kind of accident you could never predict or prepare for.

Whatever it was, I know you didn't choose it. We don't choose hardship; hardship chooses us—and it brings us to our knees. And I'm genuinely sorry for whatever you've experienced.

If you're anything like me, you'll find that when you walk in the valley of hardship, the enemy is always lurking in the shadows. Even though we experience grief and loss differently, Satan sees it all the same—as an opportunity. He kicks us while we're up and especially while we're down. But he's sneaky about it: in the midst of our pain, he'll try to convince us to use the hurt as an excuse to turn away from becoming who God has made us to be.

Might as well just walk away—it's always going to be this way.

Tell me, what kind of good God would do this to you?

Trust me, somehow this is all your fault.

It's hard not to buy the lie. The past and present pain you feel—it's real. It's real and it's deep, and I wish I could tell you it's something you can just white-knuckle your way through. It's not. Processing hardship takes intentional and tender care.

While I can't tell you when the pain will end, I can tell you that it is *never* the final chapter. And I can tell you that how you handle hardship will determine the harvest that you experience on the other side.

MISSING MOM

When I was growing up, hardship seemed to be around every corner. I went to several funerals before I ever attended my first wedding. I was constantly worried about sick family members, and I knew more about cancer than I did about college admissions. My elementary school memories are filled with waiting on my mom to finish chemo treatments before she dropped me off at school.

We don't
choose hardship;
hardship
chooses us—
and it brings us
to our knees.

She tried the best she could to make things seem normal for her two boys. After all, that's who Susan Connolly was. As a single parent, she juggled weeks packed with full-time work and our school and extracurricular activities, on top of her treatments. And she didn't allow my brother and me to do anything halfway. There were no excuses. That is, I remember being *full* of excuses, but what excuses actually stick with a single mom who's battling for her life while trying to hold together life, with her *very* full-time job at the local bank?! The answer is *none*.

This was never more true than when it came to our grades. Even though Cs technically got degrees, in the Connolly household it only meant—you guessed it—consequences. I'll never forget the Christmas that I got an overwhelming haul of good stuff—only to have *every* single item immediately taken away once my progress report came home. Not only did she take my stuff, she took my door off the hinges. How does a single mom battling cancer and enduring chemo take a door off its hinges? Probably supernaturally. I don't remember the specifics, but she got it done. The youth have a word to describe this: *savage*. Susan Connolly was savage before savage was . . . well, savage.

It was when the weekends arrived that the abnormalities of our life were most exposed. Rightfully so, my mom would sleep a lot. My younger brother and I would be left to entertain ourselves. Not to mention keeping up with the household chores. As two preteen boys with a sick mom, we'd try to get through the piles of laundry the best we could, but we were no match. The piles remained. There were blips of normalcy throughout my childhood, especially when Mom was blessed with a season of remission, but the truth is, we straddled the line of childhood and adulting regularly.

I mentioned this story briefly in the previous chapter, but let me tell you more. One Monday morning while driving to work (obviously), Mom had to pull over and call 9-1-1 for herself. She couldn't breathe. I was in college at the time, and her cancer was back with a vengeance. From that time, she deteriorated quickly; the cancer had run its course. Before they had to medically induce her into a coma, she did, however, plan her whole funeral—because that's who Susan Connolly was.

Strong. Fierce. A fighter. Always needing control. And my biggest supporter.

She finally left us on June 9, 2004.

The loss happened on a day, but I will feel it for a lifetime. It's been over twenty years, but I've experienced a thousand little deaths since then as I live my life without her. Each missed shared opportunity causes a little death in my heart. There are days I struggle to remember her voice—a little death. She didn't see me get married or meet our kids—two aching little deaths. Flipping through my old high school Bible recently, I came across a little Post-it note she scribbled me of a verse from Jeremiah. Under the verse, she wrote, "One day, you will preach." But she never heard me preach—a little death.

One of the hardest things about losing someone in this life is not being able to talk to them ever again. It would do my heart some good to call and talk to Susan Connolly today. To call and celebrate on the good days, and to have an ear or shoulder for the hard days. I'd tell her about our summer: about how I finally got to go to Togo, Africa, and that I saw her royal highness, Adele, in concert at Hyde Park. I'd

One of the hardest things about losing someone in this life is not being able to talk to them ever again.

tell her about the revival we're experiencing in our small faith community. I'd tell her about how the young boy who got Cs all the time somehow found himself writing a book to help people. She'd probably laugh, take credit, and tell me it happened all because of the time she took my stuff away. And of course, she'd be half right.

Mostly, I'd tell her that I miss her. That some days, it's hard to be without her.

BE REAL

You know as well as I do that in the midst of our pain, it can feel like God is further away than ever. We are blinded by the hurt and the grief and the anger that covers every single part of our lives. We are overcome by questions: *Why would God allow this to happen? How will I go on now that I've lost so much? Does God even care?*

It seems counterintuitive, but if we're going to persevere through hardship, our first priority is going to involve bringing those questions to him and talking to him through whatever we feel, however often we feel it.

I'm suggesting real talk, to a real God. It doesn't have to be pretty poetry. Actually, it won't be pretty. For whatever reason, sometimes we act one way toward God, but another way toward people; with people, we feel like we can be real, like we can vent and cry and rage, but when it comes to God, we have to be formal and flowery. But God isn't looking for a formal, "O God, thou who dwellest in the clouds" kind of prayer. That would actually be the opposite of why he sent Jesus in the first place. Jesus came and walked among the people for this very purpose: so that we could talk to him like a friend. Isn't that what Jesus said? We can say, "Hallowed be thy name," but we can also say, "God, how could you?" When it comes to talking to God, remember: he's after relationship and not the ritual of religion.

Talk to God in anger if you must. Cry out from the depths of your pain. He can take it. In fact, he invites it. Read the Psalms if you don't believe me. I'm sure some of my angriest, most honest prayers came after my mom died. God can take it—actually he's the only one who can take it. And he's the only one who truly sympathizes. When people say, "Bless your heart, I know how you feel," it is sometimes code for "I don't know how you feel." But God does. He lost his Son, his people turned their backs on him so many times, and he felt every single rejection deeply. He's seen it all, he's experienced it all, and he can handle it all.

If it's helpful, use the Scriptures as your guide. They offer example after example of God's people getting real with him in times of distress. Job just lets God have it (he kind of lets everyone have it). In my house, Jeremiah is known at times as the whining prophet. David cries, "God, my God, why have you abandoned me?" (Psalm 22:1, NLT). These people aren't just hurting, they're desperate. They're using real words coming from real emotions.

Don't give in to the pressure to perform in your season of hardship. As we like to say in my local faith community, we're not looking for a recital, we're after revival. Going through the motions like it's a recital won't make it better. It might not feel like it, but there's a process that's taking place in this moment. This is how we find the comfort and the truth that we really need. Bottom line, being real with God is how we will remain persistent in the midst of resistance.

> Don't give in to the pressure to perform in your season of hardship.

Being real with God is how we will remain persistent in the midst of resistance.

HEALING AFTER HARDSHIP

One of my favorite moments in Scripture is found at the end of John's Gospel. It has all the key ingredients I love about life: Brunch by a beautiful sea. Good conversation over a meal. Life re-centering. And most importantly, Jesus.

The disciples found themselves in the midst of deep heartache and loss. For three years they had followed their best friend around as they lived what most likely was the time of their lives. They left their jobs, family, homes, and comforts to follow Jesus of Nazareth. They shared meals, deep conversation, joy, and heartache. And now he was gone.

So after his death, the disciples did what was familiar—they went fishing. As they were fishing, something incredible happened: they saw Jesus walking on the beach. It didn't take long for Peter to jump out of the boat and swim to him. If you remember, it was Peter who had proudly declared that he wouldn't let anything happen to his friend, that he would defend him at all costs. If I had to guess, I bet he had been replaying a lot of *what-ifs* mentally and emotionally since Jesus' death:

What if I had chopped off a few more ears?

What if I hadn't given in to fear and denied him during his trial . . . three times?

What if I had spoken up before they put him on the cross? What if that would've changed everything?

Knowing that Peter denied Jesus—his best friend!—during his hour of greatest need, I wonder if Peter had also been carrying around the weight of responsibility for what ended up happening, and as a result was being consumed by a tidal wave of guilt. Grief and guilt can make for a nasty cocktail for the soul.

Isn't that how it can be for us, too, in moments of deep loss, tragedy, and hardship? We start to second-guess how we handled everything pre-tragedy—as well as judge how we've acted post-loss. There's always more that could've been done, said, or tried:

What if I had stayed by their bedside more?

What if I had intervened sooner?

What if we had gotten medical help faster?

*Could've, should've, would've*s are our constant companions in hardship. And the weight can be unbearable.

Which is why what follows in Peter's story is so incredible and healing. Jesus extends forgiveness to Peter for his denial, yes. But I think something deeper and far greater is happening. Their conversation also heals and frees Peter. With one question after the next, Jesus begins to restore Peter.

"Peter, do you love me?"

"Yes, Lord, you know I do."

Over and over again. Three times in all (see John 21:15-17).

Here's where the real healing starts to take place. Jesus takes the unbearable weight of responsibility, guilt, and shame off of Peter and applies a new responsibility—he tells him to "feed his sheep." That's his true responsibility. Not shame and guilt. And that's exactly what Peter did—he went on to disciple and preach and bring new followers to Jesus for the rest of his life.

If you and I are going to persevere through hardship like Peter, here's something I want to be very clear about: When it comes to unexpected tragedy in our lives, that's exactly what it is— unexpected tragedy. Sometimes what happens to you isn't your fault, and everything that flows from that horrible circumstance isn't your responsibility.

You know what *is* your responsibility? How you respond. Mental replays of false responsibility due to hardship or tragedy will only lead to more hurt rather than any healing. Put down the shame. Put down the guilt. Stop rehearsing the *should've*, *could've*, *would've*s. Instead, partner with Jesus for your healing so that you can carry what is rightfully yours—so that you can, like Peter, step into your true purpose.

THE VALUE OF PATIENCE

It's a hard truth to swallow, especially if the wounds of loss are fresh: our pain is part of the process of becoming the person God is making us to be. That promise doesn't feel good and true when you're in the thick of it, I know. But before we can actually work through our hardship, we have to root ourselves in this fact: God will use our pain for his purposes—eventually. How he plans to do this, and when, will be made known in his time.

We hear that truth, and because our pain is so great, it can be easy to just jump straight to seeking the purpose, to try to rush and "find the meaning" so that we don't have to keep processing our grief anymore. The issue with that is we stop short of full healing—and at great cost. Wounded people end up wounding people, creating more hardship and tragedy for everyone.

I do believe Satan plays a part in our hardship, regardless of what it is. But don't let him steal the abundant soul growth God intends for you to experience. Stick with it: be real with God about what you're feeling and orient yourself to the true purpose God has called you to. Does hardship hurt? Absolutely. A thousand little deaths. But you are made in the image of the one who endured the hardest of days on the cross. And that resurrection power and Spirit is available and at work for those who believe. Speaking of resurrection, for those who believe, we know death doesn't have the final word. Life does.

Because of this, we can be patient—we can trust him. We can be confident we will get through whatever we're facing. We will press through the sting of death and see resurrection. I believe so. But more importantly, our Father believes so.

God's resurrection power and Spirit is available and at work for those who believe.

Searching for Presence

When God Seems Silent

Don't let his perceived distance lead you out of what his presence led you into.

Silence can be deafening—especially from heaven.

There's a pier near where I work and live. It's .6 miles from the church and .9 miles from our front door. Very rarely do you see another soul on the way there. The dirt path to overlook the water is framed in by live oaks that have been here a lot longer than I have—than we all have.

The pier itself isn't sound in structure, but it's safe enough. Some boards are missing. Some have been re-planked. You can tell because some are more sun-kissed than others. As you step out to the end you get a panoramic view of the Ashley River.

In the distance is West Ashley. And if you stand in the exact right place, you can see the Cameron estate from the hit show *Outer Banks*. (If you know, you know. If you don't, that's okay too.)

I don't go for the fandom, but for the nature. Unique greens like you've never seen are projected off the cordgrass. I heard one time that cordgrass in the Low Country gives off the same amount of oxygen as the Amazon Rainforest. Maybe that's why being near the water is restorative in some ways.

The pier is a quiet place. The smell of salt fills the thick, still air. Every once in a while, you're disturbed by a boat or even a plane, but not often. Over the years, it's become holy ground—a sacred place. I take the flat and peaceful walk when I need to collect my thoughts. When life feels swirly. When I have a moment to take a break, I'll walk over and get much needed sunshine. Leisure wasn't always the motivation, however.

When we first moved here, I made the pilgrimage out of desperation.

CAN YOU HEAR ME NOW?

Any time you begin something fresh and new, it comes with a flare of excitement that propels you into your future. When we relocated to Charleston, there was a sense of anticipation and expectancy that filled our hearts.

A chance to establish a new home and meet new friends. And a chance to eventually establish a new faith community for the people of this area.

For me, changes like these are birthed because of a faint but certain whisper from heaven. It's a response to a leading or calling we sense from God. And usually, these times are filled with tiny little encouragements from the Father:

Keep going.

Don't give up.

Transition is hard, but so worth it.

Not only do I experience heavenly encouragement, I tend to receive creative inspiration as well—ideas or strategy or direction from God that I can use for life, both personal and professional. When doing tough things, this kind of connection is the source of my confidence. The tough tasks and times will be okay because I hear from God—often.

But that changed once we got to Charleston.

What once was a vibrant, two-way conversation turned to radio silence. Maybe I had the wrong number? Maybe God had gone on vacation, and I didn't get the auto-reply email in my inbox?

I don't know the cause to this day, but I do know the consequence.

I felt lonelier than I ever had before.

It feels important for the magnitude of that statement to mention that, on a scale of extrovert and introvert, I tend toward introvert. Middle-of-the-road solitude is what my kind longs for. But this was different. This was desert-and-wilderness loneliness— and I didn't like it one bit.

Some changes are birthed because of a faint but certain whisper from heaven. It's a response to a leading or calling we sense from God.

The experience of God's perceived silence overshadowed my belief.

The thing is, every week I stood up before a crowd of people to talk about all things God and faith. I only had things to say because he said things to me. I don't care how good of a preacher or communicator you are, that's just how it works. All of a sudden, the silence was far louder than the guiding voice. I knew God to be Emmanuel with me.[1] I knew the Logos to be the Word and the one who walked among us. I knew the Bible spoke of the power and presence of God not only being with me, but in me. Yet this promised intimacy felt fleeting. The experience of God's perceived silence overshadowed my belief.

Such a feeling of isolation blanketed my heart that I fled to the pier in desperate hopes of hearing from God there. But even my walks in that silent, holy place couldn't seem to fix me.

And I knew that if I were to continue to fulfill my responsibilities in life, I couldn't do it under this weight of doing it alone.

I SEE YOU

Nothing lights up a person quite like knowing they've been seen.

It could be they've received a note from a friend. Or an acknowledgment from the stage. It could be a text, a compliment, or even a quick DM. To receive a communication is to be told someone was thinking about you.

If this is how we feel with other humans, how much more when God communicates that he sees us?

This is one of my favorite things about Jesus. From town to town and conversation to conversation, he wanted people to know they were seen. Because if they knew they were seen, they would be convinced they weren't alone in this life.

One of my favorite examples of this is his interaction with Nathanael. Nathanael had heard the buzz about this man named Jesus from his friend Philip. The way John communicates the account in his Gospel hints that these men had been waiting for the Messiah to come, and Philip made it clear to Nathanael that he thought he'd found him: Jesus of Nazareth.

Now, Nazareth wasn't necessarily a must-go-to destination. It was more like a must-go-around type of town. And Nathanael was a little skeptical, responding to Philip along the lines of "Seriously? How good of a Messiah could this guy be if he's from the mundane town of Nazareth?" He wasn't sure about this Jesus guy.

Jesus, though, seemed sure about Nathanael. John writes, "When Jesus saw Nathanael approaching, he said of him, 'Here truly is an Israelite in whom there is no deceit.' 'How do you know me?' Nathanael asked. Jesus answered, 'I saw you while you were still under the fig tree before Philip called you'" (John 1:47-48).

Before Nathanael could even see Jesus, before he could even have the time to see if his skepticism was warranted, Jesus saw Nathanael. And not just visibly saw him. He *saw* him. At his core. With this statement, Nathanael knew he'd seen something supernatural, that something bigger was truly going on. And it produced a deep joy in his heart.

He knew Jesus saw him, always and authentically. Even when he couldn't see Jesus, Jesus saw him. From now on, he would never truly be alone. This was a marking moment for Nathanael.

If we're going to do hard things and endure hard circumstances, we need to know that we aren't alone. When we feel like we're alone, we're not. When we feel like heaven is silent, it's just taking a breath.

PRACTICAL PRACTICE

I'm always in for a good reminder from the Gospels, but what on earth are we supposed to do in real life? What are we supposed to do tomorrow when we enter into a tough circumstance and God feels silent and far, when we are thrown into deep feelings of isolation? How do we tangibly press in and keep going when we experience the resistance of God's silence?

Practice What He Preaches

One thing I've found to be really helpful is to practice what *he* preaches, not what I preach. Sometimes what I preach is based on feeling and circumstance, especially in hard times. It can be easy to let experience trump truth. Feelings are wonderful guides, but they make for a horrible god. If I get too into my feelings, it can make for a pretty convincing sermon that's contrary to what the Bible *actually* says about God's presence.

Practice what he preaches. When you read passages like Psalm 23:6, rehearse them until they restore you. "Surely goodness and mercy shall follow me all the days of my life" (ESV). All the days of your life, your Shepherd is with you. You're never alone.

When we feel like heaven is silent, it's just taking a breath.

Go Back

Anyone who hikes knows the importance of trail markers. When you are lost or alone, it's important to try to get back to the last place you were.

The same is true in our spiritual lives. If I experience a deep time of loneliness and silence when it comes to hearing from God, I've learned to go back to what was last said, the last time I heard from him. During the early years of my ministry, I had to go all the way back to the time he impressed upon me a desire to start a church in the first place: in my Toyota 4Runner on the way back from a seminary class. That memory is the light unto my soul in moments of resistance. When times got tough in our transition to Charleston, I had to remind myself of the prayer walks that gently tugged our hearts to move here. In the hard and trying days of parenting teens, I let my mind wander back to the days when they were toddlers who stole my heart. And yes, even in marriage, it's helpful on the hardest days to revert back to the whimsical days. (After all, isn't this what Proverbs 5:18 encourages: "Rejoice in the wife of your youth"?)

What did he last ask you to do? Where did he last ask you to do it? What parts of the Bible resonated with you the most in the past?

Don't let yourself become overwhelmed by what God isn't saying, and instead go back to what he last said. Allow these moments to be anchors and signposts to keep you on the right path.

Stay Put

Sadly, I meet too many people who change everything in their lives at the first experience of heavenly silence, no matter how small. They compromise core convictions and enter (or stay in) an unhealthy dating relationship rather than waiting to hear from God. They move from one city to another if God doesn't cause everything to fall right in place. Some give up on God-ordained tasks or close the doors on their dreams.

If God's voice was what prompted you to start something, let his voice be what prompts you to stop something. Put another way, if God seems to be silent, that may simply be his way of telling you to not give up. Don't try to solve the silence in your life, because it might not be what you think it is.

Listen, I know it's hard. But we can't let these painful seasons of silence cause us to give up and walk away. Instead, trust God to carry you through the hard times. Here's something I see consistently in Scripture: God leads his people in a time of wilderness so that he can meet their needs in manna moments. He leads them into a time and place where only he can fulfill their desires and longings.

The same is true for us. God's silence has a purpose: to develop a quiet and steadfast trust that God is with us *always*—especially when we don't perceive his presence.

Don't let his perceived distance lead you out of what his presence led you into.

BE STILL AND KNOW

I still make my way to the pier. In fact, when I finish writing this section, I think I'll take a walk. The way and the path to get there don't really change. Seasons make it look different. Every once in a while a house on the way

God leads his people in a time of wilderness so that he can meet their needs in manna moments.

I don't go searching for presence; I go already having the presence of God.

will boast a new addition or a remodel. But it's mostly the same. Beautiful and simple.

But unlike my surroundings, something has changed in me. I don't go searching for presence; I go already having the presence of God. I don't go and wait for God to prove that I'm not alone. I go knowing that he's with me, no matter what's said or unsaid. In fact, it's in the stillness that I know he's God (see Psalm 46:10). It's in that same stillness I know I am not alone, and neither are you.

7

A Parade of People

When Rejection Is Our Only Friend

You, like me, may know this with cruel certainty: relationships have the potential to be the source of our greatest joy—or of our greatest pain.

Close your eyes and envision it with me: the perfect relationships. You live in an incredible city with the most incredible people. (Let's use Manhattan as an example.) Everyone has an incredible job, but here's the best part—you don't really need to be there that much. Because of this everyone meets at the cutest coffee shop and just talks about life. (Let's call it "Center Perk.") The best part about it all—everyone has amazing apartments close by. Spacious and beautiful. They look like they cost a fortune, but that's okay—your jobs that you have, but never have to be at, cover it all!

If you're wondering why this scenario sounds familiar, it's probably because this is my version of the hit TV show *Friends*. If we're honest, we probably all have a vision of the perfect friendships.

Connections are established. Pursuit is mutual. Roots establish themselves deeply and securely. Growth happens. Flourishing follows. They see all of you, and you see all of them. Intimacy becomes the fruit of these types of relationships. Friends. Coworkers. Roommates. Spouse. Parent to child. No one is rushing to give you a hit TV show, but it's beautiful to behold the potential of healthy human connection in our lives. What can't you do with people on your side? Relationships motivate and sustain us.

Except when they don't.

Sometimes, instead of connection, division somehow takes over. Past or present hurts drive a wedge between you and another person. As you've probably heard and even experienced, hurt people hurt people. We begin to build walls so that we can avoid this soul-crushing pain in the future, but that only perpetuates the problem.

What do you do when you've been rejected by someone you cared deeply for? When a beloved friend betrays you or a coworker stabs you in the back for the boss's approval? That's "friendly fire," but what happens when you experience "family fire"? This supposed safe place becomes a dangerous place. How do you go on? While it can be relatively easy to overcome the sting of being snubbed by a youth sports team, how do you wade through the wounds caused by a parent, a spouse, or even a former spouse? How do you move on from these crushing moments in life in order to trust and love again?

If we are going to persist in the face of resistance, *we need people.*

You, like me, may know this with a cruel certainty: relationships have the potential to be the source of our greatest joy—or of our greatest pain. We're all imperfect people trying to love other imperfect people with what's destined to be imperfect love. But if we are going to persist in the face of resistance, *we need people.* Isolation isn't an option. So we need to figure out how to persevere in the midst of pain caused by people.

Which means, to begin, we have to look rejection in the face.

THE ROOTS OF REJECTION

I was only five years old when I first made the unwelcome acquaintance of rejection.

When my parents got divorced, deep roots of rejection dug into my soul. Though I know it was not my parents' intention, I felt unwanted by them, as though for some reason I wasn't worth staying the course in their marriage. There were many reasons they felt it best to end things, but this is how I felt nonetheless. And even though rejection in the nuclear family can cause enough hurt and heartache for a lifetime of counseling, my pain didn't stop there. "Unwanted" and "doesn't fit in" seemed to be the chords constantly strummed to make up the song of my childhood. Whether it was on sports teams (baseball, basketball, you name it) or even in our church community, rejection followed me, whispering that I wasn't good enough to belong. Even in the most welcoming and accepting places, I felt like the square peg trying to force my way into the round hole.

I quickly discovered the only way to survive was to go on the offensive—it hurt less if I hurt first. I decided to reject people before they could reject me. Have you ever felt this way? If I didn't let anyone in, I wouldn't feel left out. If I could build high enough walls in my heart and soul, very few would make the effort to climb over the wall and eventually wound me.

I wonder if I'm not alone. If you've walked this earth, chances are you've dealt with rejection. Maybe—as with me—it started in your immediate family, and rejection came from the place you should've found the most love and acceptance. Or maybe it was a friend, someone who just up and left without warning. Maybe it was a spouse. When you trust someone with every part of your heart and then rejection enters the picture, it can be devastating.

If we're going to persevere relationally in this life, especially through seasons of rejection, we have to start with acceptance. I'm not talking about accepting the rejection, necessarily—I mean we need to root ourselves in our unconditional acceptance in Christ Jesus. Let me tell you, if we are convinced we're the fully accepted child of God the Father, we can withstand the worst rejection this life throws at us. Will there be pain? Absolutely. But it won't be permanent.

Throughout Jesus' time on this earth, he received heavenly reminders that he was perfectly loved and accepted by the Father. In fact, it was audibly declared from the heavens (see Matthew 3:17). This is how God feels about you, too, my friend. Here's the most beautiful truth about our heavenly acceptance—it is unconditional. Think about this: every other relationship we have in this world has conditional variables. We must love well. Care well. Respond accordingly. We must never try to hurt the other person. But with God it has less to do with us and more to do with Jesus. We know from the Scriptures that, because of Jesus' work on the cross, *nothing* can separate you from this acceptance, that no amount of earthly rejection can take it away from you (see Romans 8:38-39).

Whether on our worst or best days, our acceptance remains unchanged.

If we are
convinced we're
the fully accepted
child of God
the Father, we
can withstand
the worst
rejection this life
throws at us.

Does this mean we won't feel the effects of rejection? Does this mean we won't be devastated if someone we trust leaves us or hurts us? No. It's just a reminder that we have balms to heal our wounds. In your pain, you'll be tempted to focus more on the rejection itself, on the circumstances and how they're keeping you from the life you had envisioned. But instead, focus on the acceptance you already have. Eventually the rejections of this world will fade in comparison to our heavenly acceptance.

"LIFERS" WHO LEAVE

What felt like gaping wounds of rejection in my childhood would prove to be only paper cuts compared to the rejection I experienced when we began our church.

Our heart's desire for our faith community was to have the pastors be participating parts of the flock as well, so Jess and I found ourselves regularly opening the doors of our hearts and home to people who attended the church. We consciously worked to develop deep relationships. We became co-laborers and friends. We bared our souls to one another and committed with all earnestness to sticking with each other through thick and thin.

I had one particularly close friend in this season. As a kid, he grew up with parents in ministry, and he shared with me the trials and tribulations he had witnessed his dad go through as a pastor. He expressed that he wanted to stay close like a brother—to walk with me through it all. I really sensed we were going to "do this" together. We all long for the friends who become "lifers." I thought this was one of those friendships.

Those pronouncements of life ended up producing only deep pain.

Sometime later, I sensed that something was off with my friend, so I asked him to coffee. (He was ghosting me before ghosting was a thing.) Eventually we met up. It was awkward from the get-go, but I chalked it up to the noisy, packed coffee shop. We eventually found seats in the midst of the standing-room-only atmosphere. As soon as we sat down, he began what almost felt like a sales pitch.

"Well, Nick, I'm so glad you were able to accept my invite to coffee."

But wait, didn't I invite him? Something was definitely up.

"Nick, I think our season at the church has come to an end. I've actually accepted a job in another city."

I was crushed. I had no idea my friend was looking to leave our church, much less that he had thought of moving away. Everything was being revealed in real time. Here I thought our relationship was *High School Musical*—we were all in this together. I was so wrong. Though it wasn't his intention, all the scabs of rejection hiding wounds I'd nursed over the years were ripped off at once.

I thought this crushing coffee conversation would be a one-off—but it became my norm for several *years*. One pastor I know called it a "parade of people." The cycle would go like this: We'd meet a new friend or couple, overcome our scared feelings of rejection and develop a relationship with them, and finally begin to trust again. And then, out of nowhere, I'd be at coffee or dinner listening to exit plans and exciting opportunities *not*

Rejection will do whatever it can to distract you from your future, but we can't let the *who* rob us of our *why*.

Instead of being deterred from the task at hand, Jesus pressed even deeper into his personal *why.*

where we lived, *not* at our church. A parade of friends would pass by, and another set of friends would follow.

Just like in childhood, I went into survival mode, building walls and isolating myself from deep friendships. But this time, it went even further: I began to count myself out. I was done with friendships. I was done letting people in.

Have you ever felt this rejected?

I remember one of the most intense moments of Jesus' life. He found himself betrayed by someone in his innermost circle of friendships. It was someone he spent most of his days with. He'd poured into this person, and still, he was betrayed. Later, Jesus stood in a garden, sleep deprived and in deep anguish over the days ahead. And yet, instead of being deterred from the task at hand, he seemed to press even deeper into his personal *why*—the mission God had given him. He didn't come to be served, but to serve and to lay down his life for many (see Matthew 20:28). His purposeful *why* was greater than the pain experienced by this one person.

Rejection will do whatever it can to distract you from your future, but we can't let the *who* rob us of our *why*. The purpose God has for you is too important. It doesn't minimize the pain you've experienced—absolutely not. But it can help you rebound accordingly. It can help you extend proper and appropriate forgiveness in due time and press on to do what only you can do on this earth. You have a unique calling and purpose.

RECOVERING RECONCILIATION

Did you catch the phrase I slipped into the last paragraph: "appropriate forgiveness in due time"? I don't know about you, but I find this is a hard reality to swallow. I'm quick to *accept* forgiveness and very slow to *extend* forgiveness. Now more than ever we are quickly offended and slow to apply grace. When we feel wrongfully hurt, we justify our hurtful responses: "They hurt me first!" We hold a grudge like we're hanging off the side of a cliff for dear life—with no signs of letting go.

We've established how people can be a source of our greatest pain, but we need to remember that they can also be the catalyst for our persistence. God calls us to relationship with him *and* with others. Which means that, like it or not, part of persisting includes working through appropriate forgiveness and reconciliation if possible. And truthfully, you'll most likely have to be the one who goes first. You'll have to be the one who pursues and reaches out.

Before I go any further, I know there are certain situations that are extenuating. They exceed human pain and enter into human tragedy. The unfathomable was done and the most sinful act was committed. What I'm *not* asking for—and more importantly what *God's* not asking for—is for forgiveness that restores a friendship or relationship as if nothing ever happened. I'm only asking you to consider how you can extend forgiveness *from* you that leads to a lasting freedom *for* you. How can you grow from resistance in order to experience the abundant future God has for you?

So where do we begin? Let's take a look at the ultimate act of forgiveness as a model: God's forgiveness of us.

First, Look Up

In Luke 15, Jesus tells a story of two sons and a father who have a family business. The younger son becomes fed up with his current life and as a result does something very culturally inappropriate: he asks for his inheritance *before* his father dies. And then he leaves his father and brother to manage the family business while he goes to the equivalent of Las Vegas to live the life he thinks he deserves.

What I'm about to say might sound like a recent country music hit, but I assure you it's not. The younger brother quickly finds himself destitute, all his money wasted on inappropriate endeavors. He ends up penniless and friendless and working a very humiliating job—tending pigs. I find almost all work respectable, but those in the crowd listening to Jesus would've *definitely* turned up their noses at this fellow's employment.

In true Jesus fashion, he inserts a plot twist: fed up and humbled by his condition, the younger brother decides to return home. As he approaches the long driveway, his father catches a glimpse of him and runs to meet him. But rather than giving him the obligatory parental "I told you so" speech, the father does something truly unthinkable—he throws a party. Not just any party, the party of all parties. The family business stops, and the feast begins.

Maybe you've heard this story a million times. Maybe you could recite it word for word, yet you still live with gaping wounds from past rejection. But what I want us to see in this moment is the reconciliation and redemption between the father and the son. What was wrong between these two people has been made right, even though the wrongdoer didn't deserve it. Jesus presents the father's unconditional and lavish reconciliation with the son as a mirror for our own lives—as a vision of ourselves being embraced by our heavenly Father. No matter what we've done or how much we've squandered, we're always forgiven, always welcomed into the presence of our Father, in and through Jesus.

When you hear what the ending of this story symbolizes, it makes you want to celebrate, right? If you're like me, it makes you want to sing songs like "Reckless Love" a little louder and with a little more gusto. How could you not? Now you understand, deep in your core, how we've been extended this same supernatural, vertical reconciliation from God. We are *forgiven*. Rather than anger or an "I told you so" speech, we get grace. In eternity, we will feast. What incredible news this is. It's life changing.

Here's the hard part. One of the fruits of truly receiving this vertical reconciliation from God is being able to extend horizontal reconciliation—the same kind of forgiveness—to others. Ouch. I don't know about you, but this is the last thing I want to do when I've been hurt.

Next, Look Around

If you have any hopes of persevering in this life and remaining persistent in the midst of resistance—especially in relationships—you have to master the art of horizontal reconciliation: looking around at those who are or used to be in your life.

It doesn't always feel good. It feels better to just spend time belting out "Reckless Love," focusing on and reveling in the fact of our transformation in Christ. Yet, elsewhere in the Gospels Jesus reminds us to value relationship over religious experience. He teaches us that, before you can even think about entering

No matter what we've done or how much we've squandered, we're always forgiven.

> **Just as there was a fight for our reconciliation, we too must fight for our relationships.**

into sacred time with God, you need to make sure your relationships with others are intact (see Matthew 5:23-24). Maybe there won't be full resolution, but he encourages us to put down the offering and deal with the offense. Or at least begin the process.

A pastor I've grown to love and learn from once shared this amazing quote about relational conflict in the midst of the family of God. He said, "The family of God shouldn't have the absence of conflict, but the presence of reconciliation in the midst of conflict." I think he's right. It's not that we're perfect people who do relationships perfectly. It's that we're imperfect people who have experienced perfect vertical reconciliation, and therefore we're able to extend horizontal reconciliation in the midst of imperfect relationships. I know, easier said than done.

Just as there was a fight for our reconciliation, we too must fight for our relationships—especially if we want to persist through the relational resistance.

ACCEPTED AND RESTORED

A few years ago I found myself at a friend's church. We were trying to deepen our relationship in hopes that my church might become a part of their church network. It was going well, but only because we knew each other on a surface level. We were taking it slow and steady. This was perfect for a guy who was trying to cover the crevices of past relational hurts.

The service went as any church service would go. There was some singing, some announcements, a sermon, and a few more songs. Someone said amen after a simple benediction was extended. My mind turned from "holy" things to my intense physical hunger.

We couldn't go just yet. We had to wait for the lead pastor to finish his goodbyes. All of a sudden I was hit with a deep sympathy for my kids who wait for me to finish at church!

Finally the pastor walked over to where I was sitting. My excited question "What are you in the mood for?!" was interrupted with a gentle and reverent "Nick, I feel like God wants to heal you from your wounds of rejection."

Surely this was from God. We'd only just met. The pastor friend had no idea about my past or present wounds at the time. My hunger immediately subsided so the healing could begin. A few stragglers joined us and prayed over me. They reminded me of my acceptance by the Father in Jesus. And they encouraged me to let go of all the relational resistance I was clinging to. I knew there would be more hurts and additional work to do, but at least I could begin again.

Consider this your starting point for healing. Receive the grace and forgiveness of Jesus. Allow it to heal the deepest holes in your heart. And when you're ready—make the call. Write the letter. Say the hard words of "I'm sorry; will you forgive me?"—even when there's offense on both sides. As you've experienced radical undeserved love, extend the same. Don't let the resistance in your relationships keep you from the harvest that's ahead if you persist. Lost relationships can be found and healed with a little bit of love. And when they are, throw the party. Schedule the celebration. Because what was lost has been found.

8 Awakened by Attack

When Satan Goes on the Offensive

If we can learn to see our circumstances with our spiritual eyes instead of just our physical ones, we'll have a fighting chance.

All time stands still when one of your children's lives is in danger. Minutes feel like hours. Hours feel like years. And every single moment they are hurting feels more insufferable than the one before.

This has never been more true than the morning Jess and I woke up to find our young daughter, Glory, seizing. Jess called 9-1-1 while I packed the car with supplies and the rest of our children. I somehow knew we would need to be ready to follow an ambulance to the hospital. As we waited, the other two kids already in the car, we prayed and prayed. And then prayed some more. Jess jumped into the back of the ambulance, and I followed closely. All traffic laws faded from my recollection. Red lights were run and stop signs were blown through . . . I didn't care.

Because we had found her midseizure, we didn't know when it started, and we couldn't predict what the extent of the damage would be. We got to the hospital hoping for relief, hoping for answers. But in reality, it took hours and a slew of medications before the doctors and paramedics could get Glory to stop seizing. Our little girl lay in her hospital bed, completely unresponsive. Doctors tried to reassure us, explaining that the brain trauma alone would cause her to sleep, not to mention the medicines working their way through her tiny little body. It would just take time—but the wait was excruciating.

Eventually Glory started to wake up, but unfortunately, her motor skills seemed to be stunted. She had trouble speaking. It was hard for her to move. She couldn't eat. Not to mention she developed a very aggressive demeanor unlike her normal disposition. And to top it off, she wasn't sleeping at all—which meant *we* weren't sleeping at all.

We were all at the end of our rope.

We had lived in the area for only a short time, but we had already developed a sweet little community, and during visiting hours they would come by and check on us. They would try their best to put on a hopeful smile.

Halfway through our six-day stay at the hospital, we had some dear friends stop by—ones who are seasoned and strong in their faith. We prayed together for Glory's healing. But after the last amen, one of them looked at us and said, "Do you think there's something more going on here?"

Not knowing what they meant, I quickly agreed. "Yes, there's obviously something going on here!" I began to list all the medical issues that could be at the root of Glory's seizures, all the potential long-lasting effects the trauma could have on my daughter's beautiful life.

They kindly listened to me rattle off my long synopsis. Then, with compassion and conviction, our friends said, "No, we really sense something spiritually dark is taking place."

And just like that, we found ourselves in the deep end of a very dark spiritual pool—and we had no idea how to swim in it.

> **And just like that, we found ourselves in the deep end of a very dark spiritual pool—and we had no idea how to swim in it.**

SEEING WITH SPIRITUAL EYES

We know that when hardships happen, it's a consequence of living in this fallen *world*. But spiritual attack goes beyond hardship. As Christians, we understand the attack we suffer is actually a casualty of being in a *war*.

I know this isn't a comfortable topic for many. But we have to be willing to acknowledge that if we are children of God, the enemy *is* going to do everything he can to keep us from God's calling. God has a very specific plan and purpose for his Kingdom on this earth. And out of his grace, goodness, and mercy, he has chosen you and me to be a part of spreading the way of his Kingdom until he calls us home. This may be news to you (and very shocking news at that), but it's true. God wants to use *you* to represent *him* on this planet.

And as I've said, that means Satan's got a target on your back.

Whatever he can do to thwart God's great plan for the world, he's going to do it. He doesn't always cause our hardships, but he definitely capitalizes on them. He's going to attack what you

> **Even though Satan works hard, God works harder. God's heart beats to see his kids keep going.**

believe about God and how you believe in God. He's going to do anything and everything he can to make you start to doubt who you are in Christ Jesus, and then he's going to top it off by trying to convince you that giving up is the only way to save yourself.

He hates when marriages stay together.

He dislikes when we have deep and lasting friendships.

He has an incredible distaste for seeing us take big and bold steps to serve God.

Satan's heart beats to see us give up so we won't experience the promised harvest God has for those who keep going, those who don't give in to his tricks and schemes. But even though Satan works hard, God works harder. God's heart beats to see his kids keep going.

If we can become aware of the spiritual battle we find ourselves in, God will awaken our hearts to see him more clearly. If we can learn to see our circumstances with our spiritual eyes instead of just our physical ones, we'll have a fighting chance.

WHEN THE ENEMY COMES

How can we learn to spot spiritual attack? Like most things in life, we can look to Jesus as a model. Fresh off of a powerful and monumental moment—his baptism—Jesus sensed he needed some time alone to process it all. I don't blame him. My baptism was a lot, and it was very normal. He experienced a dove descending and a voice from heaven! Spiritual retreat was what his heart craved and what the Spirit prescribed. Led by the Spirit, Jesus went deep into the wilderness (see Matthew 4:1-11). Some of us enter the wilderness to search for a hiking trail or two. As for Jesus, he would stand face to face with temptation.

Do You Have Spiritual Momentum?

If you have any spiritual momentum in your life, it's the enemy's job description to come after you and undo whatever God is doing. Like I said, Jesus has just been baptized. The God of heaven just split the sky and declared, "This is my beloved Son, with whom I am well pleased" (Matthew 3:17, ESV). If anyone had momentum, Jesus did. And what happens next? Satan shows up. It's the very start of Jesus' ministry—and Satan can't get there fast enough, ready to do whatever he can to quash the power of that moment.

I don't know about you, but any time I feel like I'm making progress in my spiritual life—any time I feel like God's just revealed something to me and I'm finally healing or moving forward in my calling—something comes out of nowhere and cuts me off at the knees, making me question everything. I've said it before: if you're heading in the right direction, you *are* going to experience resistance.

When we first moved to Charleston to start our church, our family experienced a deep level of attack. We had been so excited about this move, and it seemed as if God had orchestrated it all perfectly. Having only seen our prospective rental on a pixelated FaceTime conversation with my mother-in-law, when we pulled into the neighborhood and saw that there was a vacant church *right* across the street from our new home, I almost lost my mind. My heart was convinced this wasn't an accident.

I've said it before: if you're heading in the right direction, you *are* going to experience resistance.

This home held our first church planting meetings. Discipleship classes. Home groups. Leadership meetings. Women's nights. Dinners with other families. Late-night counseling sessions. You name it, our home housed it.

But soon, that home would be the cause of such chaos and fear. Our wonderful little house, in one of America's charming little cities, God's specific provision for our family—became ground zero for some sort of sick and twisted *Ratatouille*. That's right, I'm talking rats—and I'm talking *everywhere*. They got into every part of the house. We would trap and discard, trap and discard. I'll spare you the dirty details, but trust me when I tell you that it was unlike anything I've ever experienced. Shortly after the rat infestation calmed down came the break-ins. Three to be exact, two happening while we were at home. Get this—all happening on a Saturday night or an early Sunday morning before church.

If God desires faith, Satan desires fear. And our haven of a home was now rife with fear.

How could we live here? How would we ever feel safe from burglars? How could we ever have another home group, now that we knew the rats liked joining in on the prayers? We needed to stop investing in this neighborhood, forget the church across the street, and move immediately. For weeks I couldn't sleep, worried for my family's safety. Our calling and life's purposes had nothing to do with rats and break-ins, but I personally began to really doubt God in this season. *Is he for us? Obviously, he's not allowing rats and break-ins for those he truly loves.*

It wasn't pretty, but we outlasted the chaos the enemy used in our lives. We stayed in the house. We took back our land from the rats. We shored up the house to prevent additional break-ins. We fortified our house not only physically but spiritually as well. When chaos hits, remember: resistance is a sign that you're on the right track. Don't give in to fear. Persistence is possible if you're willing to not let the chaos of the moment get the best of you.

Commit, Don't Compromise

Satan comes to kill our commitment—especially when that commitment will lead to fruitful Kingdom work. He does this best through compromise. When you go back to the temptation of Jesus in Matthew 4, he was in the wilderness and committed to a forty-day fast . . . and here comes Satan. He wanted Jesus to miraculously make himself some bread to eat. Is eating a sin? No. Is it a sin for the Savior of the world to eat by way of a miracle? Again, absolutely not. But what we see here is Satan taking something desirable, something we *need* to survive— and using it to get Jesus to compromise, to stop trusting God's provision and instead take matters into his own hands.

It's the same for us. Now for what it's worth, I can barely fast for four hours without compromising. Anytime we make a spiritual commitment or move toward health and healing, we can be sure that the enemy is going to try his best to undermine it. One time, in a season of waiting, Jess and I both sensed a deep call to be rooted as a family. We both found ourselves in a cloud of depression and despair, and we needed restoration. Not only that, but we had three kids under the age of three. They needed all of us, physically and emotionally.

So, for me, it was a season of family and nothing else. Though my soul desired work with purpose in an inspirational environment, to make ends meet, I spent my days filing papers electronically. This was the furthest from my longings.

One day, I got a call from a friend with an intriguing job opportunity. I was captivated, thinking, *God has heard the cries of his people.* I was dying at my current job. My friend was in a bind and needed someone ASAP. As he proceeded to tell me more about the job, he mentioned it would involve a massive promotion in comparison with what I used to do. I would be over a team. Not only that, there was the pay. I'd move from making about twelve dollars an hour to support this family of five to more than triple that. *God really did hear my cries!!!* Then he told me he would "of course" pay for all of my expenses and anything else needed in order to make this situation work.

But there was one catch.

Even though he knew I had a young family, I would have to move two hours away—and I couldn't take them with me. Instead, I'd be on site Monday through Thursday, and then commute home on the weekends. I offered up multiple alternatives, to no avail. As we continued to talk, it quickly became clear that this was an amazing opportunity, but it wouldn't allow my obedience to God in this season. I had committed to focusing on restoring my family—and this would only be compromise.

Did my circumstances become flashier or more prosperous because of my brave and obedient "No, thank you"? They didn't. They got harder. They got more challenging. More resistance came. But as we've discussed, resistance doesn't mean you're heading in the wrong direction; it means you're heading in the right direction. And I was—I just couldn't see the fruit yet.

If you've committed something to the Lord, do everything in your power to settle in and honor it.

If you've committed something to the Lord, do everything in your power to settle in and honor it. This means staying steadfast when "greener grass" appears. Sometimes the lawn is provided to us by God, and other times it's artificial turf "grown" by the enemy. Resist the temptation to compromise your commitments to God. He sees you. The trials will cease, and fruit will grow in time.

PERSISTENT POWER IN PRAYER

I hate to confess this, but in the midst of all of the panic and the trauma with Glory's seizing incident, my mind hadn't had a spiritual thought in days. The sleepless nights. The high stress of every moment. The worry of everything from the medical issues to the new financial pressures. It felt like we were on the edge of a cliff, fighting for our lives. I was stressed, worried, discouraged, and without hope—especially in God.

I can't explain it, but once our friends helped us see with our spiritual eyes instead of just our physical ones, a new strength arose in Jess and me. We found ourselves uniting in heart and soul. We put aside the discouragement and started to focus on the spiritual realm. We couldn't allow the chaos to determine the outcome any longer—it was time to get proactive.

We asked the nurses to give us a few moments alone. We shut the hospital door to pound on heaven's door. We entered into the quiet place of prayer—loudly. We contended with heaven for our daughter. We asked for the enemy to leave her alone. We asked for healing. We asked for a new outcome. We asked for sleep—for her and us, as neither of us had slept in a week. We asked for wisdom. And most of all, we asked for the darkness to flee. What we thought was ten minutes of spiritual prayer was actually an hour. We prayed together over our daughter.

While we prayed, Glory writhed and squirmed, almost as if she were in deep pain. But when we said amen, we opened our eyes to a peacefully sleeping little girl. The power of prayer had led to a calm moment which would turn into our first night of sleep in a long time—for all of us. The next morning, I woke with a start, and a little blur was running around the room.

It was our daughter.

As I write this, I know you may find this hard to believe, but I promise I am telling the truth. She went from having no motor skills and being unable to speak and unable to eat to running around the room asking if she could have food. The doctors went from talking about home care and rehabilitation to one more night of medical supervision, followed by discharge. We had just witnessed two things I'll never forget.

Spiritual attack.

And a miracle.

In situations like this you will be convinced you have no spiritual authority and you've simply been caught in the undertow of the moment. Nothing could be further from the truth. In Christ we have power to pound on the doors of heaven in prayer. We are not victims of Satan; we are victors in Christ.

In Christ we have power to pound on the doors of heaven in prayer.

The Fog Rolls In

When Depression Blocks the Sun

He died so that you can live. Let me say that again: he died so that you can *live*. And not just exist. Thrive.

There's a famous Greek phrase that's persevered through history. It's simple but profound: "Know thyself."

Here's something I know about me. I need water.

I'm not talking about hydration, although that is true. I mean I need to live by water—and I'm not talking about any artificial lake either. I'm talking about God-made, God-inspired bodies of water that refresh the soul. I've lived in the middle of the country—it didn't work. Something didn't take. I know me and God knows me—I need to live by water.

By God's grace, Charleston has scratched that itch for my soul. We've got rivers, harbors, oceans, and even an occasional marsh. But the thing about living by water is that during the "in between" seasons here in the Low Country, a dense fog creeps up from time to time.

Not as often as in the Bay Area, but enough. Sometimes it lasts for a moment. Sometimes it lasts for a while. Oftentimes it's difficult to see and navigate through. We have a major suspension bridge here in Charleston connecting the city to the suburbs. During the right conditions, it can hide itself to convince you it doesn't even exist. And once in a while, during some of the heaviest of fogs, life must come to a standstill. Everything pauses until the conditions to proceed are right again.

A physical fog really can be quite debilitating, but an emotional fog—a fog of the soul—can be even harder to wait out.

NAMING THE FOG

A stubborn fog seeped into my life one time. It came in as most fogs do—gradually, over time. Almost unnoticed, until I couldn't really see clearly.

It started during the time I mentioned briefly before, when we moved 3,000 miles away from family to serve at a maternity home. The recession came. Finances were tough. We had to hustle to make ends meet. We found ourselves involved in an unhealthy church, which caused us to be unhealthy. We didn't know it until it was too late and the damage was done. And then our time there was done. God was turning a page, and we made the move back home to the Southeast.

Jess bravely took our three kids ahead of me on a plane—I would finalize our life in Seattle and be only a few days behind her. I'll never forget our first phone call after her arrival. She'd just finished a much-needed nap, and when she woke up, she had no idea where she was. That's the best way I can describe our state of mind: disoriented. We couldn't see anything. We couldn't feel anything. The heavy fog had settled in. And it wasn't going anywhere.

Once you know what something is, then you can begin the plan of healing and restoration.

We tried rest. We tried retreat. Some dear friends even gave us access to their beach home. But this time, even the water couldn't restore us.

We were near family finally. That didn't help. We had sunshine again (sorry, Seattle). It didn't warm our hearts. Our kids were growing and becoming these beautiful parts of our lives. But we were too comatose to truly see it.

Our wonderful environment was at odds with our inner unease. A lot of good was happening around us, but it was almost as if it couldn't penetrate our souls. Eventually, friends would give Jess and me the word to describe the fog we were experiencing: depression.

And it was in the naming—gaining language to understand the fog—that we were able to see a little glimpse of life again. Once you know what something is, then you can begin the plan of healing and restoration. Hopefully and eventually.

LIFTING THE FOG

Have you ever felt this way? I believe depression—and further, thoughts of suicide—to be a *major* form of resistance. But unlike the other forms of resistance we've talked about up to this point, it's a totally different ball game.

Rejection at the hand of hard relationships, that's an outside force beyond our control.

Spiritual attack, that's circumstantial.

A crack in the foundation of our faith usually starts with an outside crisis that causes internal chaos.

But depression and thoughts of suicide—this kind of resistance comes from within. That's why it feels so real and final. It's almost as if this is how it should be and always will be. There's a feeling that rises up inside, pushing you to give up on life itself. To give up on everything and everyone, forever. It's a voice from within that sounds like God, but it is furthest from the heart of your Father.

Anytime you experience moments like this, you feel all the different emotions—but stronger. There's guilt. *I hate that I feel this way.* Then there's anger. *How could God let me feel this way?* Then hopelessness. *I will always feel this way.* And the nail in the coffin—shame-filled despair. *This is who I am now.*

In recent years, the degree of shame and stigma surrounding depression has decreased, so we talk about it more. But it's actually not a new emotion. In the ancient texts of this world we can see some who struggled with the fog like we do today—but especially in the Bible, where we find human experiences that encapsulate all of human emotion.

The Bible doesn't really support the notion that we should just button up our emotions.

In some Christian circles today, emotional stoicism is seen as the only appropriate response to any circumstance. The truth is, when you really get into the pages of the

Bible, you see God's people expressing tears, celebration, anger, questions, faithlessness, despair, discouragement, victory shouts, violence, jealousy, comparison, and yes—even depression. Long story short, the Bible doesn't really support the notion that we should just button up our emotions.

I can't fight alongside you physically, but I want to fight for you in the spiritual realm. My hope is to give you some encouragement from the pages of Scripture and to show you some small steps you can take to lift the fog.

OUT OF THE PIT

When you start to dig in, you'll see the Scriptures don't just address mere surface-level depression, but also moments of suicidal depression. One situation that stands out is what happened to Elijah right after he confronted the prophets of Baal (see 1 Kings 18). In that situation, God showed up in a mighty way—sending fire from heaven—to make it very clear to the nation of Israel that he was real and wasn't playing around. But now everyone wanted Elijah dead.

One person specifically—Jezebel, the evil wife of an evil king—devoted her life to seeing the task accomplished. When the word got back to Elijah, he did what I would've done: he literally ran for his life. Because sometimes that's what depression does: it convinces us fleeing is better than fighting. Picture Elijah in the wilderness, alone and afraid, as depression started to get the best of him. Here's how the Scriptures recall the moment: "He came to a broom bush, sat down under it and prayed that he might die. 'I have had enough, LORD,' he said. 'Take my life; I am no better than my ancestors'" (1 Kings 19:4).

How did Elijah get to this deep and dark place? He withdrew. Maybe you've reached this moment before. Maybe you are there now. Sometimes when we withdraw, we unknowingly choose isolation. Don't get me wrong, I love a good introvert moment, but sometimes the thing you want most is not the thing you need. Even though this feels like the right move, it quickly can become the wrong move if we stay isolated and alone.

If this is where you are, I want to take a moment and encourage you. Elijah was a powerful man of God (see James 5:17). There are things he did that we might think could only happen in our favorite Marvel movie: He healed. He prophesied. He made it stop raining for three and a half years. Then he made it rain again. He even called down fire from heaven. And he, this powerful man of God, still struggled with dark days. You and I are in great company if that's where we find ourselves.

So how did he get out? How did it get better? What happened that allowed him to lift the fog and move forward in his life?

Sleep and Food

First of all, there were a few practical physical things that helped Elijah—and I think they might help you too. The narrator tells us, "[Elijah] lay down under the bush and fell asleep. All at once an angel touched him and said, 'Get up and eat.' He looked around, and there by his head was some bread baked over hot coals, and a jar of water. He ate and drank and then lay down again" (1 Kings 19:5-6). So we see that Elijah started with sleep and nourishment. If we aren't sleeping well, we will struggle eventually. I used to not value this wisdom, but eventually the "I'll sleep when I'm dead" mentality catches up with you.

It's the same with eating. I am not a nutritionist, and this isn't a health book, but I do know what goes in our bodies physically can affect what comes out emotionally. We've all seen someone become "hangry." It can be funny once or twice, but eventually it can really inhibit the abundant life God has for you.

The Whisper of God

After Elijah experienced physical provision, he experienced God's presence. He traveled to Mount Horeb, the mountain where God spoke to his people at the time. In my own experience, making the arrangements to spend time with God becomes the front line of the battle with depression. It's where the war is fought. Really, it's a war of internal voices—will you listen to Satan's or God's? My most intense battles with depression became that way because an internal voice—and if it was really bad, a demonic internal voice—would become so loud. It would shout shame and condemnation, and even tell me to do things that were contrary to health and life.

I know you've been alone a lot, but you probably need more alone time.

You shouldn't tell anyone that. Just keep that buttoned up on the inside.

I bet God loves them more than you.

Life is bad, and you should probably just escape—or end it.

Notice how it went from reasonable to unreasonable? Rational to irrational? That's what the voice of the enemy does. He starts small to get his foot in the door. And once invited into the living room of your soul, that's when he does his "best" work.

Making the arrangements to spend time with God becomes the front line of the battle with depression.

A gentle whisper
makes me
want to lean in.
A harsh voice
makes me want
to turn away.

Recently I had a conversation with someone who told me this happened to him. What started as negative thoughts became more aggressive, angry, and unrelenting messages over time. For two years he fought a voice that, at his darkest moments, was telling him, "Just kill yourself."

If this is where you're at, look at what happens to Elijah on that mountain. He went to the mountain because he was desperate for anything to happen. Rather than experiencing "anything" he received abundance. God tells him, "Go out and stand on the mountain in the presence of the LORD, for the LORD is about to pass by" (1 Kings 19:11). First came a massive wind. Surely that's how an all-powerful God would reveal himself. Then came an earthquake. The same, right? That has to be God. Next, he experienced a fire! But God wasn't in any of those things. Finally came a whisper. *That* was God. The gentle and quiet whisper.

Why on earth would God use a whisper to speak to Elijah in a great time of need? The world can be such a harsh place, always shouting and grabbing my attention. The enemy is the same—loud and insistent. Sometimes I just need a gentle voice telling me it's going to be okay. To speak quiet peace over my current circumstance. To tell me, "Head this way," when I don't know what to do next. To impart gentle courage, when all I feel is fear.

A gentle whisper makes me want to lean in. A harsh voice makes me want to turn away.

The more I walk with God, the more I realize he's not a bully. He doesn't push us into anything. That wouldn't be love, right? Love allows the freedom of choice. That's how you know it's real love. You don't love what you *have* to do, you love what you *get* to do. God speaks gently to Elijah, leading him out of

> There is purpose that will be born out of the current ashes of your life.

his depression by reminding him of our next two thoughts—Elijah has both purpose and community.

Direction and Purpose

Once Elijah hears the whisper, God has his attention. In 1 Kings 19:15-17, God gives Elijah direction and purpose, telling him to head back the way he came and anoint several chosen leaders. This voice of direction is key—I struggle the most when I feel wanted the least. Purpose makes us know we're wanted. God has something for us to do on this planet. Remember, the greater the resistance, the greater the confirmation—you're heading in the right direction. Our lives are too important to allow depression to dominate us or sidetrack us.

You and I were wonderfully and purposefully created. And not only that—we were bought with a price. When Jesus died on the cross, he deemed your life worth giving his own life for.

He died so you can live. Let me say that again: he died so you can *live*. And not just exist. Thrive.

There is purpose that will be born out of the current ashes of your life. The enemy's harsh voice will try to convince you otherwise—but not God. One whisper from him and you will be flooded with wonder and excitement about the days ahead.

You are loved more than you know. You have more purpose than you realize. Receive that purpose, and plan to live your life, not end it.

Community

Lastly, God has one more word for Elijah: "Anoint Elisha son of Shaphat . . . to succeed you as prophet" (1 Kings 19:16). This is a call for companionship—though I'm sure Elijah sees it as a leadership opportunity. "Go find Elisha and develop him." But what if God was really saying, "Go find Elisha; you need a friend." I'm often guilty of this, thinking I'm going to help God and help someone else, while God is simply trying to help me.

Multiple times in the passage Elijah expresses that he is alone and the only one following God at that time (see verses 10 and 14). Isn't this what depression does? Makes us believe no one gets us or understands us? That no one likes what we like or cares about what we care about? It might feel true, but it's not. There are so many people and relationships ahead of you, on the other side of this fog—and most of the time, in the fog.

Good people help us see what's good, right, pure, and true when everything looks gray and uncertain. They are the lighthouse on the shore, and we are the boat tossed by the winds and waves in the midst of a dense fog. But the purpose of any good lighthouse is to help keep you safe from danger, to help you find the harbor where you eventually dock.

A good friend helps you find your way out of a gray and intense fog.

And as always, don't be afraid to seek the help of trained professionals. They provide a different kind of essential community—and they are good at what they do because God has equipped them so. Most importantly, seeking help doesn't make you less spiritual.

His depression was a part of his story, not the whole story.

THE SUN IS COMING

Eventually Elijah would rise out of his fog of despair. His depression was a part of his story, not the whole story. The same will be true for you. You are worth it. And so is your purpose—why you've been placed on this planet.

When I started to write this section, there was a dense fog over our city. As I finish, it's gone, and the sun is shining. I don't believe that to be an accident. I believe it to be a sign or message for you and me. The fog eventually lifts. The sun shines again. This is the way of nature and creation. This is the way of the Father. And this will be the way for you too. Don't give up just yet. You are too important, and your calling is too great. I think so, but more importantly God thinks so.

The Slow Cooker of Our Souls

When God Says Wait

10

Waiting is the preparation of the person for the promise.

I hate waiting.

I know we're supposed to cultivate patience and embrace the wait, but can I be honest? I loathe waiting. I've never met a line I liked. You could put me at the most magical place on earth, and I would still despise lines. Everyone in my family loves Disney, but I avoid it at all costs. Grocery store lines even do me in. In fact, we've had to pause shopping at our beloved Trader Joe's because there's always a line . . . to even get into the parking lot. Forget about it!

It's not just waiting in lines, though. The human experience seems to be about just . . . waiting for things to happen. Online shopping, restaurant reservations, Taylor Swift's next album. Even streaming services—once a major stride for our civilization in the reduction of television wait times—now have regressed to releasing episodes weekly.

But none of that compares to waiting on God. That's when the stakes feel highest—and that's when it's most difficult to be persistent in resistance. We wait for a dream or a longing, a need for healing, fulfillment of a calling, clarity in uncertainty, provision for a problem—the list goes on. Our hearts are filled with high hopes in the beginning. But over time, if opportunities don't develop as expected, deep shame and regret can take over, leading to a crushed-hopes hangover.

Why did I try that?

I must have heard God wrong.

Well, that was a big bust. I am so embarrassed!

The world would tell you to get on it. To solve by your own efforts whatever you've been waiting on to happen. "God gave you elbows—use some of that elbow grease!" Satan whispers, "God's not going to do it—let me help." It's a tempting siren song. Waiting can allow us the beautiful opportunity to move into a deeper union with God—or it can sometimes make the wheels of our faith develop a wobble.

The more I get face-to-face with people and hear the darkest parts of their stories, the more I can see the devastating impact of unanswered prayers and unfulfilled dreams. Waiting is a huge area of resistance—and it causes people to give up daily.

If waiting is a part of life—and even more, a part of our walk with God—how can we do it in a way that draws us nearer to God, rather than pushing us further away?

CHANGE YOUR PERSPECTIVE

One of the hardest things about waiting is it reveals so much about us at our core. And some of that revelation isn't pretty. Waiting reveals our vulnerability. It reveals our lack of control. It shines a light on our deepest longings and desires and exposes what we truly value.

If we're waiting to find that special someone to spend our lives with, we may have to grapple with the tender places of our hearts, like our need for intimacy, possible identity struggles, and feelings of loneliness. Waiting in traffic, on the other hand, can really pull out some deep-seated impatience in our hearts, exposing a lack of compassion and empathy for our neighbor.

Maybe most of all, waiting brings to light where we actually place our hope. Sometimes when I get tired of waiting, the revelation is that I'm really getting tired of God and I'd rather have my own way over God's plan and purpose for my life.

If we are going to learn to wait well, our perspective shift needs to start here: with remembering who God is.

If you identify as a follower of Jesus, remember we are connected to the only one who has the power to make anything happen in this world. The only one. Do we truly understand how incredible that is? God, who has ultimate authority over this world, who never makes a mistake, who can move mountains with his breath, is intimately connected to our lives. He can change this world in an instant. If we weren't followers of Jesus, how would

Waiting reveals our vulnerability. It reveals our lack of control. It shines a light on our deepest longings and desires and exposes what we truly value.

What if we saw waiting as the spiritual privilege that it is?

we have hope that anything would truly change? God knows our hearts and loves us so deeply; we can comfort ourselves by remembering that, even when it doesn't feel like it, he is on our side (see Romans 8:31). We *get* to wait on him (see Lamentations 3:25-26).

What if, instead of throwing a spiritual tantrum when the waiting gets long (as I often do), we could start from a place of gratitude? What if we saw waiting as the spiritual privilege that it is?

Waiting is not a have-to. It's a get-to. And I don't know about you, but for me, that changes things.

When we can change our perspective on waiting—when we see it for the blessing that it is—we move from being entitled to elated that God would give us anything at all. And he promises us more than just anything—he promises us the desires of our hearts if we delight in him (see Psalm 37:4).

WORTH THE WAIT

Here's something that has helped me when it comes to waiting: remembering that often the wait is in proportion to the promise.

I've got some bad news and some good news. The bad news first: just because God's on our side doesn't mean that it's not going to be a long wait. *Ouch.* I know it isn't easy: we've all got these dreams in us, and we want to see God move. We want to see miracles happen! And the longer these dreams take to come true, the more disillusioned we get. The wait just feels so long.

But here's some good news: the wait will be worth it.

Let's consider Abraham and Sarah, who were promised a son, even though they were barren and in a "seasoned" time of life. An heir plus land plus more descendants than the stars is a huge promise (see Genesis 15:1-5). And because of that, there was a long wait, one that didn't end with the birth of Isaac. It was fulfilled over the course of many generations.

And let's not forget the greatest scriptural example, our Savior, Jesus Christ. The people of God collectively awaited the birth of the Messiah for thousands of years! And now, we, the people of God, are waiting for his return! He's the biggest promise God has made to us. And even though his return is taking a while, I think we can all agree—Jesus is worth the wait.

So if you're struggling while waiting for God to work, take heart: sometimes, the greater the promise, the greater the wait.

THE PROCESS OF BECOMING

There's another thing we need to remember while we wait: the wait has a purpose. The fact is, God's more concerned about who we are becoming than about what we're waiting on.

This seems so counterintuitive to us, especially in this day and age. After all, aren't we supposed to keep our eye on the prize? But God sees the bigger picture, and while we are waiting, he keeps one eye on the promise and one eye on the person—that is, who we are becoming.

According to God, our character will always outweigh what we're waiting on. In fact, waiting is the process by which we're formed

The fact is, God's more concerned about who we are becoming than about what we're waiting on.

more into the image of Jesus. It's how the fruit is produced in his people. It's how he advances his Kingdom.

Does God still care about the promise? Absolutely. Remember, he has graciously extended these promises to us out of love and care and a desire for partnership. But the waiting—the waiting is what prepares us to be able to handle the promise in the first place.

Waiting is the preparation of the person for the promise. Even though it feels like nothing is happening in the physical while we wait, plenty is happening in the spiritual. God is moving. God is working. God is preparing the soil of our souls to grow and fulfill a beautiful promise—that is, the deep longings and desires of our heart. But the work starts with the person. It starts with us.

Remember Abraham? God did deep work in Abraham's heart during the waiting. Yes, Abraham got his son. But when you read Hebrews 11, he's known more for his faith—the internal work. The work in the waiting prepared him to be the person God created him to be. In the wait, Abraham learned to trust in God's plan rather than his schemes.

LONGINGS AND LEADINGS

God loves to fulfill our longings, so don't confuse his "not now" for "never." Have you ever thought about where your desires and longings come from? If they are good and holy, they came from him! Have you ever considered that the longings you have might be more than just a pipe dream? Maybe it's time to uncover some buried dreams and desires that you've talked yourself out of. Maybe it's time to see them for what they are for. They are from God and for the world.

And if you know the dream but don't know the time frame, maintain your perspective. The very fact that we get to wait on anything is such a blessing. Remember, waiting is proportional—the greater the promise, the greater the wait. And don't forget, God is working on you as a person while you wait on your promise. This is a time of preparation so you will be ready to steward the promise.

Don't let moments of waiting coerce you into giving up, or even worse, attempting to force the outcome you want before it's the proper time. Don't take the promise out of God's hands. His timing is good. Waiting on God isn't easy, but it sure is worth it.

Don't take the promise out of God's hands. His timing is good.

Part III

Choosing Persistence

Outlasting the onslaught leaves
behind two remnants: guilt and grit.

Guilt for the times we've given up
prematurely and walked away.

Grit for the battles we
currently face.

You might have heard it said that
"everything happens for a reason."

I believe that reason to be
choice. Specifically, the choice
to fight back with persistence.

Grace for the Give-Ups

The message of grace says we aren't what we do or don't do—we are who we are because of Jesus' work and identity.

I didn't always believe in persistence.

If you were to ask me about my past employment, you'd find out I've held the most random jobs. I've worked retail, coffee shops, data entry, electronic paper filing, and construction. Once I was a property manager for HOAs. All that meant was I would be the one writing you letters if your lawn got too out of control or if you erected an unsanctioned and unapproved fence. And then you would call me and give me a piece of your mind. I did stained-glass repair once. We'd take these beautiful glass windows and gently disassemble them to repair cracks in the middle. It took such care and patience. Often I'd have to start over after cracking a piece of glass unintentionally. One thing I remember about that job was coming home with itchy hands due to tiny little shards of glass getting stuck under my skin.

It might sound like I'm an eclectic Renaissance man. But if you dug a little more, you'd see I couldn't stand resistance. At the first whiff of hard times, relational conflict, boredom, fear of messing up, or any other issues at work, I would get out of Dodge—quickly. There always seemed to be greener grass elsewhere.

During the first years of marriage, Jess and I moved ten times in nine years. Often the move was rightfully inspired, but other times we just didn't want to stick out a tough situation. We were always moving on to something better. The possibilities of new cities and people always inspired us.

I'm sure you'd agree—there's a lure to the new. It's hard to not be excited about what awaits us when change is in the mix.

TRANSIENT TIMES

Isn't this just how life is? Transient lifestyles seem to be the norm now. Gone are the days when you worked one job for forty years until the pension kicked in, lived in one city, at one house, and attended one church. (You may currently be saying to yourself, "Own a home—must be nice!")

I recently read that the best way to move ahead in your career is to move from job to job every year and a half. The article said that if you change jobs, you'll receive more compensation and promotions than if you stayed at one job and faithfully moved up the ladder. In this case, the reward is found only when we relocate.

One of the hottest trends I've noticed on social media is people living in vehicles. They will outfit anything and everything as a residence so they can travel anywhere they can drive. I'm sure you're picturing a roomy Sprinter van or massive RV with all the bells and whistles. I've seen those. But I've also seen some of the tiniest little cars being used for this purpose. The other day I came across someone who was living out of their Toyota Prius! True story.

If traveling in cramped vehicles isn't your vibe, you can travel by plane to anywhere you want—all while holding a job that's remote. What a brave new world this is. We have the ability to live anywhere but nowhere all at the same time.

After all, if there's zero commitment, there's zero regret.

THE GUILT AND GRIEF OF GIVING UP

Traveling around the country in a van can seem whimsical and carefree on Instagram. And switching up jobs to get ahead in life may work for you. But there are aspects of life that hold a little more weight, where persistence is incredibly important. Let me say it this way: when we don't persist in those areas, it can be incredibly wounding, both to us and to those we love. If you've made it this far in the book, you'll observe we've talked a lot about not giving up and what it takes to press through resistance. But what if you've already given up on something very important in your life?

You've walked away from your marriage.

You've deserted your kids.

A big dream became difficult, and you walked away. Now you're left working a nightmare job that's snatching your soul away—day by day.

> When we don't persist, it can be incredibly wounding, both to us and to those we love.

Or maybe the friendship that once withstood the test of time crumbled due to disagreements.

What I've noticed in my life is that when I give up on the good stuff, a deep grief and guilt settle in as a result. It's the hangover that's left after the hard decision is made and things come to a halt. The *what-if*s and *should've*s, *could've*s, and *would've*s start to take over and talk back.

Guilt left unchecked usually becomes shame. How do you know when that's happened? When what you've done becomes who you are.

If you divorced—you feel like that's all anyone ever knows about you, and it will be forever and always.

If it was a failed profession, "failure" starts to solidify as your identity. And if it really settles in, you're not sure you'll ever try something brave and bold again.

If a friendship was cut short unexpectedly, you now believe that you're bad at friendships. Damaged goods even.

Do you see the difference? The grief over "This is what I've done" turns into "This is who I am."

So what's the only thing that can stop the sting of giving up?

Grace.

GRACE THAT COVERS THE GIVE-UPS

As a pastor, I've heard all kinds of stories about people's pasts. And being a pastor in the South, there's a term I hear all the time: *backslid*. I'll treat this moment like a spelling bee and use it in a sentence: "Well, I was walking with the Lord and then I got to college. I *backslid* a little bit. But now I'm coming back to the Lord."

Every time this topic comes up, I graciously nod my head, knowing exactly what the speaker means. We've all had a season where we've walked away from God—or at least inched a toe across the line. But usually in this scenario the speaker is emphasizing behavior, not belief. What's interesting is that when you read the Scriptures, this term is used interchangeably with *faithlessness* (see Jeremiah 3:22 and 5:6). Therefore, it would seem the term has more to do with the object of our trust than with what we've done. To God the source of our identity should be our belief in him, rather than what we've done or not done rightly.

Back to grace. Sometimes we'd rather our behaviors (whether good or bad) determine how we feel about ourselves. If I am crushing it and doing well, then I feel great about myself. If I am struggling and feel like a failure, I'm down on myself. To connect the dots, if you've given up on something in life and are experiencing a deep shame and guilt, you've chosen to view and define yourself based off that one moment rather than off the message of God's grace.

The message of grace says we aren't what we do or don't do—we are who we are because of Jesus' work and identity. And what seals us in this reality isn't the right actions; it's the right belief—faith.

Which leads to another piece of good news— the "great exchange" (see 2 Corinthians 5:21). Jesus took our past, present, and

> **The source of our identity should be our belief in God, rather than what we've done or not done rightly.**

The bigger the impact of our mistakes, the bigger the covering of grace.

future mistakes on himself. And we receive his righteousness. This means we are in right standing with God, in Christ Jesus, because of his persistence on the cross—and in spite of our lack of persistence in a certain situation.

This is the grace of God that covers all your past "give-ups" and "give-ins." In fact, the bigger the impact of our mistakes, the bigger the covering of grace.

Now this might make some of you very uncomfortable.

Nick, people can't just do what they want and then expect God to love them fully and cover up their mistakes.

Sorry, but that's exactly how it works—he takes all of our transgressions away (see Psalm 103:12). And not just "away" like we'll be forced to deal with them at another date or time. Away, away. Permanently. The verse actually says, "as far as the east is from the west."

I know it doesn't make sense. And for this Enneagram 1 perfectionist—with a slight hint of "older brother"—I couldn't be more grateful for this grace.

God cares about whether or not we stick it out and remain persistent. He does. That's why he's given us the power of the Holy Spirit. But his love for us isn't swayed by whether or not we stick it out in every situation.

One more thing about grace. What if you were the one given up on? As I mentioned before when we talked about vertical reconciliation and horizontal reconciliation, sometimes it's far easier to receive grace than to extend it. I desperately want you to receive the necessary grace from God for any give-ups in your past, but what do we do with those who have given up on us? Maybe it's time to extend some grace to them also. Yes, I know that's easier said than done, but if we are going to accept grace freely—we will have to extend it freely as well.

Get rid of the guilt. Say goodbye to the shame. Yours and theirs. Embrace and extend the grace. And watch the grief of it all melt away.

MOVING FORWARD WITH PERSISTENCE

Don't move on too quickly. Wait. There's more. Because once we take part in this exchange—when we give Jesus all our good, bad, and ugly, all the times we've given up when we should've remained persistent, and he in turn gives us his right standing before God—we are able to then stand before God. We trade our capacity for his capacity.

When we think about persistence, here's what that means: every time I want to quit—when I want to give up and let go—I remember that giving up is what *I* would normally do. This is my capacity apart from Christ. But now I have more: I have a new capacity by the power of the Holy Spirit. My lack of persistence is replaced by Jesus' perfect persistence.

And Jesus? He's never given up on anyone or anything. He faced difficult people, and he kept going. He experienced betrayal and hurt, and he pressed on. When it came time for him to lay down his life in the most horrific way—death on a cross—after some deep anguish and prayer time with his Father, he remained persistent.

My lack of
persistence
is replaced by
Jesus' perfect
persistence.

His persistence is now our persistence.

This is now who you are.

This is now who I am.

We are the persistent ones.

We need not shudder at the first sign of resistance any longer. We don't need to worry about whether we have it in us to power through the hard times. There is grace to cover our mistakes. We have the Spirit to empower us to persist through any and every kind of resistance.

THE GOOD NEWS OF GIVING UP

If you've given up, that's okay. I don't know about you, but I find that good news. And I hope you'll agree.

What you've done isn't who you are. The past or present decision to give up isn't a pronouncement over your future. In grace, you're known not as the one who gives up but as the one who now can keep going. And if you don't know how you'll keep going, that's okay too. In God's Spirit you have everything it takes.

12

Fighting Back

The trick to persistence is finding a way to outlast the onslaught of resistance.

When I am in a season of overwhelming resistance, I'm ultimately faced with two choices: I can throw a pity party for myself or I can learn the mechanics of a new skill: persistence.

Up until this point in the book, we've been talking a lot of theory, really grounding ourselves in our understanding of how God has empowered us to persist through hard times. You have to build a good foundation before you can safely live in a nice house. But we can't stop there—merely acknowledging resistance and its many forms doesn't magically make for a persistent spirit.

If only it were that easy.

The trick to persistence is finding a way to outlast the onslaught of resistance. To steal a phrase from Eugene Peterson, we

Not every tool in this toolbox is going to work for you—and that's okay.

need "a long obedience in the same direction."[1] Do you want to give up because you've structured your life for a sprint, not a marathon? Your race might make for an exciting moment. You'll probably have great stories, but your strength will give out before you ever get close to the finish line.

What I want to offer you in this chapter is a persistence toolbox of sorts. It's a bit like my junk drawer at home—filled with a bunch of things that aren't necessarily related, but all serve a valuable purpose. And like a junk drawer, there are things you might need today. But it's mostly items you keep but will need in the future. These are tools I regularly use to fight back, to persist in the midst of resistance. Not every tool in this toolbox is going to work for you—and that's okay. Take what you need and leave the rest.

STRETCH YOURSELF PHYSICALLY

A few years back my wife and I were sitting around with a group of friends on Thanksgiving. Everyone was talking about a half-marathon they'd all be running in a couple of weeks. My wife is the runner in our family. I am not a runner. It's the whole running-for-a-long-time thing that gets me. And the early mornings. I've never seen a race start at a reasonable time in the morning. Of course, I'm a big supporter of my wife running. But me? I avoid running like my kids avoid a vegetable whose taste can't be concealed with ranch dressing.

Midway through the conversation, I heard my name being mentioned at the volume of a loud whisper. This got my attention. My wife and a friend were discussing whether or not I would consider running in the race with them. Yes, the same half-marathon that was a couple of weeks away. My wife, in the midst of a crowd of our friends, turned to me and said, "Nick, *would* you run the race with me?"

I felt called out.

I don't know if it was the sugar high from the Thanksgiving cinnamon buns I'd recently downed or the peer pressure, but without thinking I quickly responded, "Sure! Why not?"

She was both stunned and excited all at the same time. And I was—just stunned. What was I thinking?

I run the risk of sounding redundant, but I need to make something very clear.

I. Don't. Run.

I hadn't trained. Sure, I worked out regularly. But running any type of distance? Absolutely not.

And the race was only two weeks away.

Once our friends left and we continued on with our Thanksgiving, Jess and I made a plan. I'd run one mid-range distance of about five miles on a Wednesday, and if I survived the five, I'd run ten miles with her on a Saturday.

Wednesday came. We did it. She killed it, and it didn't kill me. Immediately I was filled with the thought, *I didn't know I could do that!* A glimmer of confidence started to shine. The following Saturday, we set out to run again. This time ten. The last few miles were brutal, but at the end of it all, I was still standing— barely. I did it.

I was flabbergasted.

I'll never forget the morning of the race. Even though it was December, it was about 70 degrees with 100 percent humidity. And then there was the music. Who thought it was a good idea to start the race this early with loud music and a local DJ?

But one mile at a time we finished the race. To my shock—I'd done it.

Here was my takeaway from that experience (and no, it wasn't a 13.1 sticker on my vehicle): there was more in me than I'd realized. If I could make it through a half-marathon, what else could I make it through?

There's more in you than you realize. Find some new physical challenge—one that you want to take on. For some unexplainable reason, physical toughness breeds spiritual toughness.

Now, of course, all of our physical capacities are going to be different, and I want to be sensitive to that. The challenge doesn't have to be big to anyone but you. It could be a walk, a run, a personal lifting goal, or it could be courageously persevering through life despite a physical setback. The point is the movement and the challenge: because God can use each one of our physical challenges to grow our spiritual muscles.

Resistance is both physical and spiritual. And there's more in you than you think.

MAKE TIME FOR SABBATH

Persistence is impossible without the regular practice of Sabbath. If you do not stop, you will not be able to keep going.

I get it. It's hard to stop. To stop is to sacrifice control. And we all love control. Maybe it's just me? Perhaps this book finds you launching into something new and exciting. You are living the dream. Why stop when you've worked so long to get as far as you are?

Or maybe you are in the middle of a battle for your life. How on earth are you going to stop fighting—after all, if you don't fight, who will?

Persistence is impossible without the regular practice of Sabbath. If you do not stop, you will not be able to keep going.

But the truth is, the dream doesn't belong to us. The fight was never ours to win in the first place. It's all God. He gave you the dreams in your heart. He's the only one who can win a battle. Throughout Scripture, one of God's main points of contention with his people was connected to the observance of Sabbath. Whenever the Israelites started to believe they didn't need him and they were perfectly fine without him—that was when his people strayed from him. When you pick up God's story in the Gospels, Jesus calls people back to a new kind of Sabbath—a new kind of rest (see Matthew 11:28-30). One that was free from the burdens of the rat race, whether that race be one of religion or one of trying to keep up with the culture. Because he promised rest and retreat from both, he became wildly unpopular. People don't like it when other people mess with human tradition, religious or cultural. And that's what a Sabbath does. It kicks against the goads.

First, it's important to talk about what Sabbath is and isn't. Sabbath is a twenty-four-hour pause from the regular pace of life to enter into an irregular pace of the Kingdom. It is a ceasing of activity, control, and our compulsion to play God and try to solve all of life's problems. I can attest, some of those problems will still be there post-Sabbath. But I've also found that some

Sabbath is a twenty-four-hour pause from the regular pace of life to enter into an irregular pace of the Kingdom.

of life's problems? They do begin to clear when we commit to Sabbath. It's almost as if our stopping leads to solutions.

What Sabbath *isn't* is a twenty-four-hour period to catch up on work or do what you couldn't do while working. A great example of this is allowing your favorite streaming platform to wash over you while you tune out from life's stresses. Listen, I get it. But that's numbing, not Sabbathing—and numbing doesn't solve anything. In fact, it actually *subtracts* from rest. A Sabbath isn't about simply replacing work but rather about replacing work with that which is spiritually restorative.

What brings restoration to your soul? Maybe it's a walk with God? Maybe it's an incredible meal at a new restaurant with your favorite people? Could it be a new recipe you've been dying to try but haven't found the time? Creating is far more restorative than mindlessly consuming.

By pausing for twenty-four hours, you declare that you are not a better lord over your life than God himself. Pause. Rest. Sabbath. Because it's only when you stop that you will be able to keep going.

PRIORITIZE PRAYER AND ABIDING

About eleven years ago I came across a missionary called Andrew Murray. I respect Andrew so much that we named our last child Cannon Murray after him. His life appealed to me for a few reasons. First, he ministered mostly in South Africa, and even though I've never been, I have a deep appreciation for all things South African. Additionally, I learned he would ride horseback from town to town in order to pastor people. Talk about a pioneer—literally! But most of all, there were his writings.[2] He wrote so much about practicing a personal time of intimacy with Jesus.

Specifically, Murray's writings on John 15 show a deep understanding of the importance of abiding or remaining in Christ for a fruitful life. What do I mean by abiding or remaining? The best comparison I have to this is spending time with my wife. When we share a day together or go on trips, I am constantly aware of her presence. I talk to her. She'll talk back and I'll listen. There are also times when we don't speak and just enjoy each other's presence.

Here's the most remarkable aspect of this scenario. When I spend time with my wife, it produces the deep fruit of intimacy, connection, and health that allows us to be even more fruitful in our God-given responsibilities. So as we parent, we parent from intimacy and deep relationship—abiding. When we go to our jobs, we work out of the security of our relationship with each other. After all, nothing gets me off of my game more quickly than a marital dispute. I need to make it right, before I am right at work. Bottom line, our healthy relationship together is the precursor to a productive life.

The same is true with my relationship with Jesus. Sometimes I talk to him. Often, I try to listen and give him a chance to speak. He is always present with me because the Holy Spirit lives in me. This is what it means to abide or remain in Jesus. Our intimacy with Jesus leads to an abundantly fruitful life. Because we tend to this relationship, it tends to produce fruit in our lives. We produce in our God-given life responsibilities, out of personal intimacy with Jesus.

Our intimacy with Jesus leads to an abundantly fruitful life.

This concept is quite countercultural if you think about it. To most of us, productivity comes from activity—the more you strive and "crush it," the more successful you become. But this is the complete opposite of what

Jesus says in John 15. Productivity actually comes not from what we do, but who we spend time with. Jesus makes this connection: "Apart from me you can do nothing" (verse 5). True fruit comes only from being faithful in our time with God each and every day. Daily time with God allows us to persevere through each day. Daily faithfulness with God leads to a life lived faithfully for God.

Think about some of your best human relationships. Any relationship we nurture will be nurturing to our souls. Here's something that might be hard to hear: we're careful to make time for the things we truly care about. So why do we fail to make time for God? I don't mean to sound harsh, I just really care for your well-being. Additionally, I care for your ability to remain persistent in the midst of resistance. Resistance will win if you don't have a close relationship with Jesus. Our relationship with God can't be sustained by mere acknowledgment of his existence or occasional attendance at a local religious gathering. To be honest, very few things can be sustained without regular participation and attention.

If it's ten minutes, fifteen minutes, or even thirty minutes—give God what you've got. He'll take care of the rest. After all, isn't that what Jesus shows us when he feeds the multitudes? He takes what little bit we have, and he multiplies it. He just wants what we have. It could be a conversation while we take a walk on a ten-minute break from life's pressures. If it's a morning or afternoon commute, give it to him. If it's a ten-minute pause between Whac-A-Mole naptime sessions with your kids, that's more than enough.

If you're waiting for the right conditions—the "perfect weather"— to connect with God, you will be waiting for a long time. After all, the best connections happen in the midst of storms.

Time with our heavenly Father as his children shouldn't be a complex equation. It's as simple as this: time plus receptive availability equals profound intimacy. Here's something simple I've done every day for a few years, and it's worked really well for my soul. I have a "GPS journal," and it is the guide for my time with God and honestly, my life.

Gratitude. Prayer. Scripture.

First, gratitude. I start by tuning my heart and reciting what I'm grateful for. A lack of gratitude will result in a lack of persistence. Gratitude acknowledges God is moving, even in the toughest seasons. It's an acknowledgment that he hasn't given up—and as a result, you won't either.

Next, prayer. Talk to God. Ask him for answers. Ask him questions. Let him talk back. Personally, I'm still working on getting better at that last part. Never would you go out to coffee with a friend and make requests of them for an hour straight, never pausing to listen. So, let God talk back.

Finally, Scripture. Scripture corrects the soul. It encourages the soul. Scripture is one big letter from God to his kids, telling us to keep going—we're almost home. If you don't read the persevering pages of Scripture, you will have a hard time persisting in life.

GPS. Gratitude, prayer, and Scripture. Possibly a little cheesy—but highly effective.

Like I said earlier, we make time for whatever is important to us. Abiding in Jesus is important. Make time for it. If you do, resistance will come, but victory will be yours.

PRACTICE "BENEVOLENT DETACHMENT"

I first came across the phrase "benevolent detachment" from John Eldredge, but some have said it has deep roots in Ignatian traditions. In his book *Get Your Life Back*, Eldredge says he has this phrase he repeats throughout the day: "I give everyone and everything to you, God."[3]

What a profound statement. And as it is with most profound statements in life, it's easier said than done. Something I've noticed in my own life is that I'll let go of persistence if I'm holding on to all of the resistance in my life. If I'm holding on to life's issues, I can't hold on to God. I can't hold on to what he's asked me to do.

It's easy to feel like we need to be a referee for God in this life. We're ready to blow the whistle at every social media post, infraction, and life choice of those inside and outside our social circle.

"You can't do that."

"You shouldn't believe that!"

"This is right and that is wrong."

While I'm a firm believer in truth, I also have firm beliefs as to how truth should be applied. I can't be responsible for how everyone lives and applies truth in their daily lives, or whether they apply truth at all. If I do, I won't be able to live out *my* daily life. As Joshua says, "If serving the LORD seems undesirable to you, then choose for yourselves this day whom you will serve, whether the gods your ancestors served beyond the

If I'm holding on to life's issues, I can't hold on to God.

Euphrates, or the gods of the Amorites, in whose land you are living. *But as for me and my household, we will serve the LORD"* (Joshua 24:15, emphasis added).

I think Joshua was able to remain persistent in the midst of resistance because he released everyone and everything to God and chose to carry only himself and his household. If you approach life with an attitude of "everyone else and their household," you will burn out and ultimately give up. It's impossible to hold your life and the lives of others around you. You must stop playing referee.

You might be thinking, *Nick, this just sounds like an excuse to be passive.* It's not. I don't know what's more caring and loving than actively releasing someone into the caring hands of our Father. In fact, I'd argue it's probably more passive to handle things on your own without giving them to God. This also includes releasing life's burdens that are unsolvable by us—and unfortunately unsolvable at all. That's the point.

We have to be able to live in the tension of both "God will solve this" and "we might not see resolution this side of heaven." We must keep our eyes on Jesus, the Persevering One, and regularly practice benevolent detachment if we are to live a faithful and persistent life in the face of resistance. Remember John Eldredge's phrase: "I give everyone and everything to you, God." Say it first thing when you wake up. Say it often throughout the day. And most importantly, repeat it to yourself and God when your head hits the pillow.

SOMETIMES I AM MY OWN RESISTANCE

I've heard there are two types of people: pioneers and settlers. Deep down, I identify more with being a pioneer. Part of being a pioneer means we are skeptical of the well-worn path. "Everyone

We have to be able to live in the tension of both "God will solve this" and "we might not see resolution this side of heaven."

is doing it" automatically means we won't be doing it—whatever "it" is. And if I'm really feeling my stubborn streak that day, I'll reject anything and everything for the sake of finding my own way.

> "Yeah, I've heard breathing oxygen is required for living, but I don't think that will work for me. That's not how I'm wired."

> "I'm a one, wing nine . . . that's not how it works for us."

While I respect the pioneer in us all, sometimes a belief like this keeps us from experiencing breakthrough in hard and heavy seasons. If we're quick to say, "It won't work for me," we can miss out on good and godly wisdom. Necessary wisdom.

Recently I came across the spiritual conversion story of the man called Saul who later went by Paul—one of the pioneers of the early church. It was a very powerful moment in Acts 9 that changed his life and the Kingdom of God forever. Later on, Paul retells the story: "We all fell to the ground, and I heard a voice saying to me in Aramaic, 'Saul, Saul, why do you persecute me? It is hard for you to kick against the goads'" (Acts 26:14). In other words, "Why are you hurting yourself through your stubbornness?"

If we're quick to say, "It won't work for me," we can miss out on good and godly wisdom.

Everything in this life requires true and honest discernment. But if you're feeling a little bit like Saul, take a moment to pause and reflect. What tools for persistence might God want you to add to your junk drawer? Different tools may be most helpful in different seasons. But no matter the season, God remains with you and for you. Don't throw a pity party. Practice fighting back. Try it out. See what sticks. Maybe there are some new tools you can add to the toolbox? Shift what doesn't. Seasons change, therefore application does too. But God remains with you, and he is for you—especially in seasons of persistent resistance.

I'm confident you'll discover you're created for "long obedience." And long obedience is found in our daily decisions. Practice these behaviors on the good days and especially on the hard days. In times when you feel like you can't fit in one more thing, I pray you'll discover these practices are worth it. But more importantly, your persistence is worth it.

13

Dream the Dreams

Resistance might defer the dream, but it doesn't destroy the dream—or the dreamer.

I've been told I'm a dreamer. I say it that way because to me, it's just normal. To others, it's apparently not normal. My wife and others close to me remind me often that their minds don't work this way. How big of a dreamer am I? Let me paint you a quick picture.

Jess and I were getting ready to welcome our first child into our family. After Jess's many heroic hours of painful labor, the doctors decided it would be best for her to have a C-section. Now, C-sections are quite common these days, so it's very important to not lose sight of this fact: C-sections are *major* surgery. Like all first-time parents, we were scared, overwhelmed by all the information and by how quickly everything was happening. I won't go into the details, not because you can't handle it, but because I can't handle it. I'm confident the nurses were more worried about me than about my superhero wife, taking bets on whether I would pass out or make it through the procedure without running out of the room. Needless to say, I'm not a frequent medical-TV-show-watcher—you can keep your *Grey's Anatomy*.

Stressed and hyped on adrenaline, we finally reached the last room before the operating room. Everyone was moving around like bees in a beehive: each person had a job, knew their place, and did their task with urgency. Our job was to sit and wait while they finished their preparations. And as you may know, when you are forced to be in one place for a long time, you get a lot of time to process. For some, processing involves planning; they lay out every single detail of the coming event to feel a semblance of control.

But me? I go straight to dreaming.

Once we were all settled and ready for the procedure, Jess turned on a wonderfully curated playlist she had made on her iPod while we waited (you read that correctly). Right before she started her favorite songs, she and I had a moment. We locked eyes as if we were in a rom-com movie. Jess told me how much she loved me and how excited she was to meet our first child—a son. And what a great father I was going to be.

And I lovingly looked back into her eyes and said . . .

"WE SHOULD MOVE TO NEW YORK CITY TO HELP PLANT CHURCHES IN MANHATTAN!!"

DON'T QUIT THE DREAM

Dreamers gotta dream, right?

Except when I couldn't.

Dreaming about the future produces a daily faith.

Difficult times have the ability to kill the dreamer in us all.

As you've read, the dreamer in me would be continuously tested in the coming years. Difficult times have the ability to kill the dreamer in us all. In fact, I think that's what the enemy of our souls wants. If we stop dreaming, we essentially stop living. If we stop dreaming, we cease to hope. And the enemy loves when people are hopeless and lifeless.

Have you ever experienced a moment like this? Where your once-hoped-for dreams have been lost—decimated—in the heartaches of life? You've forgotten why you exist or how God might want to use you—and even who you were created to be. When we find ourselves lost like this, it can be so easy to lose sight of who we are and where God was taking us in the first place.

In one of Paul's letters to the Corinthians—one of the many churches he helped start—he voices this feeling we all have in the midst of the ups and downs of persistent resistance. Here's what he writes: "Though we experience every kind of pressure, we're not crushed. At times we don't know what to do, but quitting is not an option. We are persecuted by others, but God has not forsaken us. We may be knocked down, but not out" (2 Corinthians 4:8-9, TPT).

Quitting isn't an option. And even though we've been knocked down, we are going to keep going. But how will we keep going?

I'll tell you what we won't do: we won't stop dreaming. In my life, I've been able to persevere in the resistance because I've refused to stop dreaming about the future God has for me. This is what hope is—faith in what's to come. In fact, dreaming about the future produces a daily faith. Through every trial and hardship in life, God kept whispering to my heart through the Scriptures: keep dreaming.

DREAMING IS BIBLICAL

Before you dismiss what I've said as flowery, fluffy, and even fantasy, I need to remind you: Dreams are biblical. Dreams are spiritual, spurred on by the Spirit of God. In God's Word, we find many different accounts of individuals who have been spurred on by dreams in times of resistance.

I can't help but mention Joseph, whose story is told in Genesis 37–48. Even as a young man, he dreamed often about what God was going to do in his life. He was born into a big family with lots of brothers who gave him the hardest time out of jealousy. Soon the normal brotherly jousting turned dark. One day they decided enough was enough and they wanted to get rid of Joseph. First, they threw him into a cistern while they decided what to do with him. Then, they sold him into slavery. Joseph would eventually end up in a foreign city serving in the house of Potiphar—the captain of Pharaoh's guard.

But even though he was far from family, he wasn't far from God.

As with every good movie, there were many twists and turns. Just as Joseph was settling into his new role, he was wrongfully accused of a crime and thrown into prison. But God was with him in that prison. Even in that place, the dreamer was able to hold onto his dreams and even help others with their dreams. Eventually, all things dreaming would be his ticket out of his terrible circumstance and into a new season of life.

God protected him, watched over him, and gave him more and more favor. He rose above all the resistance of his life to become

The pain from hardships doesn't kill the promises of God.

one of the most powerful and prominent men in Egypt. This is the kind of stuff movies are made of.

He never stopped dreaming, and as a result, he saw the dreams come to fruition.

"Nick," you say, "that was just one guy. One isolated event."

Maybe. Maybe not.

Many years later, after the Exodus and taking the land of Canaan and lots and lots of kings, the Hebrew people were forced to live in captivity and exile for about seventy years. Throughout the time away from their home, God would speak to them through prophets. And those prophets would be communicating the visions and dreams God showed them about what was to come. In fact, these dreams were what allowed some of them to persist through resistance.

Eventually God would fulfill those dreams and bring them back home. Which is why the book of Psalms says: "When the LORD brought back his exiles to Jerusalem, it was like a dream!" (Psalm 126:1, NLT).

They dreamed of this day. God promised. They kept dreaming. Why? Because the pain from hardships doesn't kill the promises of God. Resistance might defer the dream, but it doesn't destroy the dream—or the dreamer.

And last but certainly not least, the Scriptures present us with John's revelation of what's to come at the end of it all. In a dreamlike vision, God showed John the blessed things that await us and are to come. He mentions many things that will be tragically hard and must take place, but he doesn't leave out the

> **God is going to resurrect your dream in ways you might not expect.**

dream of what's to come. He says, "He will wipe away every tear from their eyes and eliminate death entirely. No one will mourn or weep any longer. The pain of wounds will no longer exist, for the old order has ceased" (Revelation 21:4, TPT).

RESURRECTION OF IT ALL

My friend, no matter what kind of resistance you're facing today, *this* is the promise I want you to cling to: God is going to resurrect your dream in ways you might not expect. That is what allows us to dig in and hold on a little while longer. We can remain persistent in resistance because relief is surely ahead of us. We hold on because God is holding on to us.

It takes time. And patience. But then, out of nowhere, the death-of-it-all turns into the resurrection-of-it-all. We begin to see clearly. We begin to get pep in our step. We learn to trust God for the present and the future—again. We know he's brought us through the nightmare so we know he will bring us through to the dream he's given us.

Dreaming isn't an escape from the pain; it's a passage into the future God has for you. It's exercising an expectancy that there will be resurrected life on the other side. It's expressing a faith that believes hurt and hardship won't be the finality of your life and one day God will see you through to a new day.

Little by little. One bold step followed by another bold step. Dreams I thought I had buried deeply into the hard soil of my soul, God resurrected. If he did this for me, he'll do this for you too.

One way to see yourself through to the other side of extreme hardships is to keep dreaming. Maybe the dreaming takes place on a cancer floor of your local hospital during chemo treatments. Maybe you find yourself having recently buried a loved one, and there in the depth of your grief, the seed of a dream remains. Or maybe you find yourself in a position similar to the one I was in, nursing the wounds of fresh disappointment due to crushed dreams—and even though it doesn't make sense, the dreamer in you just can't quit. Whenever you're able and willing, dreaming will be your secret spiritual weapon to navigate the hardships of life (see Joel 2:28 and Acts 2:17).

You may want to give up everything else, but please, don't give up dreaming. Dreaming isn't an escape from the pain; it's a passage into the future God has for you. It's brave. It's the exercising of an expectancy that there will be resurrected life on the other side of the pain. It's the expressing of a faith that believes hurt and hardship won't be the finality of your life, and one day God will see you through to the other side. As Psalm 126 concludes, our hurts will one day lead to a harvest—and our tears will be the rain needed for the growth ahead.

14

The Harvest Ahead

**There will come a time
when your faithfulness
will be met with fruitfulness.**

I never want to assume, but I wonder if you might be thinking something like this:

Don't lie to me, Nick.

I'm in too much pain to enter into a worthless chase to ease the suffering. I need to know it's worth it to keep going. I need to know the future hurts will reap something. I need to know my labor isn't in vain.

When my marriage feels dead.

When another promising love interest has only led me to heartbreak and disappointment.

When I hate my job.

When I feel the pains of a dream-turned-nightmare.

When I feel the sting of betrayal and rejection.

When my world is just mundane, despite my dreams.

When I'm in a deep fog of depression and dark thoughts.

I've mentioned it a few times, and I'll say it again: there is a harvest that awaits you on the other side of hard times. There's a payoff that's bigger and better than the pain of the moment. But that payoff can only be accessed by choosing persistence.

Here's the beautiful thing about God: he wants to be seen. He wants to reveal himself to you and me. He reveals himself to us in our wounded wanderings. He also makes himself known in the form of a reward on the other side of resistance. It's one of the ways he loves to reveal himself.

Let these words witness to your soul: "Let us not become weary in doing good, for at the proper time we will reap a harvest if we do not give up" (Galatians 6:9). You can take that to the spiritual bank. There will come a time when your faithfulness will be met with fruitfulness. If you are still unsure if you can trust these words, please consider: the verb meaning "to reap" occurs twenty-one times in the New Testament.

There is a harvest that awaits you on the other side of hard times.

Maybe that's not a lot to you, but I'll tell you, it's enough for me.

If we embrace, no, choose this mentality of persistence—we will reap a harvest.

KEEP SHOWING UP

Paul tells us that "the one who sows sparingly will also reap sparingly, and the one who sows generously will also reap generously" (2 Corinthians 9:6, NASB). In other words, we need to keep showing up. If there's a limit to our persistence, there might be a limit to our payoff. Sow by showing up. Sow daily. Sow often. Reap generously.

You might wonder how long it will be until you reap the rewards. And I don't have the answer. I do know that timing is everything when it comes to reaping. If you think about it, this is how the natural agrarian ways work. You till the soil—sometimes it feels like permafrost. You plant seeds. You show up each and every day—especially when you least want to. And then, one day, the conditions change. The right time is mixed with the right rain and sun, and suddenly, harvest springs forth. (I believe God wants us Trader-Joe's-shopping people to know this and believe it to be true.)

"Springs forth" is exactly how God works. After all, this is what he reminds us through the prophet in Isaiah 43:18-19. One day we find ourselves in the wilderness of it all. In a desert drought that leaves us thirsty and hopeless to find life. A wasteland is what it feels like, but God isn't wasting one moment. When the conditions are at their very worst, God will break through with his very best. Harvest and life all at once.

Sometimes it comes in the form of a just-enough-for-today harvest, and every once in a while it comes in an enough-for-a-lifetime harvest, all in one day. A breakthrough. One day there's dirt, and the next there's a vine with fruit. You saw a wall, and the next day, the wall ceases to exist. Why does God do this? Is it because we've finally done enough, we've finally done it right?

I don't think it's as much about our goodness as it is about his goodness.

He is a good and wonderful Father. He delights in rewarding his children. This is what Jesus wanted to communicate in Matthew 7 when he was teaching his disciples about prayer and said, "How much more will your Father in heaven give good gifts to those who ask him!" (verse 11). There's a good Father in heaven who desperately wants to give his children good and wonderful gifts, rewards, and payment for their persistence. I think that's the point of all of Scripture, to reveal who he is and why he's the only one worth trusting.

And because of this, we can trust him, trust that as we persevere we will see a payoff—a reward for our persistence.

THE REWARD OF RESTORATION

Another question you may have is this: *Will we receive the fullness of our reward here on earth?* The writer of Hebrews addresses this question: "These were all commended for their faith, yet none of them received what had been promised" (Hebrews 11:39).

There are rewards and prayer requests we unfortunately won't see answered this side of heaven. There are deep desires that will only be fulfilled in eternity by the perfect presence of our God. "Face-to- face" will be the only solution to our fractured and hurting hearts in this life.

Which brings me to what I said earlier. There will come a moment when you face a certain form of resistance where the only solution is restoration. Where the only solution is simply Jesus. This is the path along which God is taking you and me

I don't think it's
as much about
our goodness
as it is about
his goodness.

in life. Sometimes we focus on the payoff and promise—but he's concerned about the process. To gain this perspective and walk this path is to step into maturity. It is the ultimate persistence. To finish this life in preparation for the next.

So what's the reward waiting for us in the next life?

First we will finally be at a cease-fire with resistance. There will be resolution for our souls. The pain and suffering will be no more. Even the need for persistence will be no more. There won't be a need to fight because you will have finally won the good fight. There will be a cease-fire and the war will be over.

This is how John, the author of the book of Revelation, pictures this moment: "I heard a thunderous voice from the throne, saying: 'Look! God's tabernacle is with human beings. And from now on he will tabernacle with them as their God. Now God himself will have his home with them—"God-with-them" will be their God! He will wipe away every tear from their eyes and eliminate death entirely. No one will mourn or weep any longer. The pain of wounds will no longer exist, for the old order has ceased'" (Revelation 21:3-4, TPT).

This is the restoration awaiting us. Perfect companionship, dry eyes, and full healing.

Not only does God promise restoration, he promises heavenly rewards too for those who persist. This is why Jesus says, "Be glad, for your reward in heaven is great" (Matthew 5:12, NASB).

At this point, you might be thinking, *Wait. Is Nick saying some of us will get larger rewards than others? Isn't that contrary to the gospel message? I always heard nothing could affect my relationship with God. I can't take anything away or add anything to it. The reward is the same for all.*

You're right. On our worst and best days, we are fully loved and redeemed. This is salvation—which comes only through the Savior's work on the cross. But salvation is different from divine dividends received in the next life.

Jesus says again: "The Son of Man is going to come in the glory of His Father with His angels, and will then repay every man according to his deeds" (Matthew 16:27, NASB). And the determination to remain persistent is an incredible deed.

A "well done" life here will earn the words "well done" in heaven, and that's a great reward.

A TEAR-STAINED HARVEST

Until that day we fight. In sickness and in health. On the good days and especially the hard days. When we're smack-dab in the middle of our wilderness wandering. If we're waiting on promise and fulfillment, we will stay the course. We will trust the process. And if we're living in the days of fulfillment and promises received—we will be on guard even more. We will remember the Old Testament warnings about squandered blessing and prosperity. Most of all, we will stay faithful and close to the Faithful One. We will choose persistence in the midst of the overwhelming resistance life throws our way. We know that every hard day has its purpose on the path toward the promise.

> We know that every hard day has its purpose on the path toward the promise.

> **And even on our worst days, we know our tears aren't wasted but will be used to water the ground to one day produce a harvest.**

And even on our worst days, we know our tears aren't wasted but will be used to water the ground to one day produce a harvest. The crying will be accompanied by laughing, since we will know that one day there will be no more tears—or as the psalmist says, "Restore our fortunes, LORD, like streams in the Negev. Those who sow with tears will reap with songs of joy. Those who go out weeping, carrying seed to sow, will return with songs of joy, carrying sheaves with them" (Psalm 126:4-6)

It might feel a little crazy, but to me, this is how you know you're doing it right. You are remaining persistent in the midst of resistance. Resistance isn't going anywhere, but neither are you. "Don't give up just yet" is the way forward. Page by page. Step by step. Day by day.

BLESSINGS AND BATTLES

I still want to give up sometimes.

Of course I do. Like I told you at the beginning of our time together, the feeling you have—the deep desire to just burn it down and walk away during a difficult time—I can't fix that. It's here to stay. It's the world we live in. In this world, we have resistance.

And I'm not immune. Just because I've committed to a life of persistence in the midst of resistance doesn't mean I don't continue to experience trials, that I don't question what God has for me to do on this earth.

Our faith community just celebrated ten years in Charleston. We've had good days, and we've had bad days. God is building something beautiful, and sometimes that comes at the cost of some broken pieces.

My family, too, is still in the hard days of it all. The kids are young. So is our marriage—seventeen years young. I say "young" because people have been committed to their pets longer than we've been married. Until our marriage has outlived Paul the parrot, we've still got a lot to learn.

Blessing and battles.

Like clockwork, resistance comes in all its different-but-familiar forms and flavors. The enemy is boring and a one-hit wonder— all his attacks start to sound the same.

It would be so easy, even after all these years of persisting, to give up on it all. To let the hard times get the best of me. To put in my two weeks' notice.

And yet.

And yet, I remember these truths: That if I befriend resistance, I can practice persistence. That I'm a child of God—and this resistance? It's only a sign I'm headed in the right direction. That there will be a payoff if I can just hold on. The hard times will cease, and then harvest will follow. This is the way of life. This is the way of this world. And this is the way of the Father.

And then one day we will be with him. And he will be with us. Eden restored. Resistance won't be present in this new place. Persistence won't be needed either—only presence.

Then we will be home. But until then—don't give up just yet.

Acknowl-
edgments

I'll start with the writing portion of this journey, then I'll address my life.

This book is the fruit of a faithful team.

Jenni, thank you for taking a chance on me. You are incredibly wise and a force for good in the publishing world. Jess and I are SO grateful to be a part of the Illuminate family.

Liz and David, thank you for helping me get the words out in the early days.

Sarah, I'll never forget our first call. I left the Zoom and immediately begged God to let me work with Tyndale. Thanks for partnering with God in that prayer.

Jillian, I can't believe we did it. Not only did we complete the task, we completed it in the gauntlet of life's resistance for both of us. Thank you for your persistence, wisdom, and edits. You made my words make sense. This book is your book too.

Debbie, you held up my arms to get to the finish line. Thank you as well for the wise edits.

Libby and Dean, what a beautiful book y'all have created.

And now life. Who we become is always connected to the people in our lives. It has been the grace of God to have key people in my life who've guided me through some of the deepest valleys and up some of the highest mountains. In fact, I know I am where I am today because of the people God has surrounded me with.

I'll start with my immediate family. My mom was one of the feistiest, hardest-working persons I know. Her love for my brother and me was evident in all she did. She gave us so much more than we should've had in the circumstances we found ourselves in. It's a little death knowing you won't read this, but so much life knowing others will get to hear about you. Thank you, Mom.

Dad and Gwen, thanks for all your love and support. Dad, thanks for being willing to throw the ball and take us go-carting. For checking on us and sending the birthday love.

Leland, thanks for being a great brother and checking in on us. Even though we grew up together, it feels like we're still growing up together, and our conversations bring me great joy.

Bradford family, thank you for loving us as your own. Some of my favorite days as a kid happened at the Bradford house. I miss Christmas Eve.

Marilynn and David, thanks for saying yes to God and birthing Forest Hill Church. It was the incubator of my foundation of faith. Roger, I've never told you this, but I lied straight to my mom's face about the Pittsburgh Project trip. I told her we had no upcoming trips and I didn't need to go anywhere over the summer. She marched me back in, and you told her the truth. That truth led to my salvation. Thank you.

Mike B, you came next and put up with a LOT of my shenanigans. Middle school Nick was the worst, but you made it the best it could be.

Robbi, I had so much teenage angst. So many crazy dreams and desires. I just wanted to serve God but didn't know how. You were gracious in every conversation. Patient with every bad decision I made. Thank you for walking me through books of the Bible and other books of wisdom. I'll never forget the book of James and talking about decision-making and the will of God in the corner of Starbucks. Thank you also for giving me my first leadership opportunities. And for marrying Jess and me. Janet, thank you for sharing your husband. I am who I am because of your generosity with his time.

Jason, Kelly, Beth, Felipe, and Jamie, thank you for your faithful spiritual guidance and devotion. I still look up to you all. Lyle, Andrew, Julius, Amy, and Kalle, what wonderful friends you are to me. Your friendships got me through some of hardest years of my life.

Simpsons, y'all as well. Miss you all dearly.

Anthony, thank you for giving Jess and me a chance to cut our teeth in ministry together. That time birthed our desires to serve God as one.

Laura, Steph, and Mere, we love y'all dearly.

Naeem and Ashley, thank you for letting us jump on the dream in Charlotte. I've always admired your faithfulness and love for others.

Whites, Claytons, Schneringers, we miss you all dearly!

Paul, thank you for awakening the desire in my heart to plant a church. And for letting me preach my first-ever Sunday sermon. I still have the Wade Boggs card.

James and Stacie, thank you for giving us a soft place to land post Seattle. And for loving us well through Glo's emergency.

To the Fort Wayne crew, thank you for giving me a chance to be a pastor. God did a wonderful forming and pruning in my heart there.

I'm forever grateful. Arnolds, thank you for staying in touch and making the yearly journey down to South Carolina. It is one of the highlights of my year.

Sam, Britt, Ben, and Kayla—thank you for saying yes to Charleston. The early days of Gospel Community/Bright City were hard, fun, and beautiful. The fruit we've experienced over the years has been of your brave yeses.

Ain't no family like the Bright City family. *All of you.* It has been a special slice of the heavenly Kingdom on earth for me. Tyler, Kbeau, Arthur, and Gabby, thank you for sticking with us through it all—the incredible days and the hard days. To the fearless leaders, Ellery, Justine, and Anna, you round out an incredible staff with Gabby and Deb. Thank you for your prayers, support, encouragement, and faith.

Pastor Michael, thank you for always being there. Your counsel has been invaluable. Your love and prayers have sustained me through the good days and the hard days. You always show me the Father's heart, and I'm forever grateful.

Mac, I'll never forget our bridge walk. It saved the church and my time in ministry. This book was birthed partly because of that day. You are always so kind and generous with your time. And you always pushed me not play victim but see every obstacle as an opportunity for growth—when all I wanted to do was whine and complain.

Gibson, Deb, and Caroline, God has given me such a wonderful gift in my in-law family. I married up in EVERY way, and that includes you all. There would be no marriage, family, ministry, and book without your love over the years. I truly hit the lottery.

Walters family, I love you all dearly. Josh, thank you for your love and friendship over the years. I look up to you. Katie, thank you for "throwing the couch." My life is different because of that night in every way. And the ways you love Jess and me so well. Thank you both for the years of fun and intimacy. The future is bright if you guys are around.

Elias, Glory, Benja, and Cannon, I am SO grateful for EACH of you. Elias, you essentially made me a father. I am in awe of your leadership and character daily. Glory, you are a walking miracle. Don't ever forget it. You are fierce and loving all at the same time. You have such a strength, and I can't wait to see how you use that for God's glory. Benja, what gifts you have. Intelligent, kind, and a lover of music. I pray God continues to make your ways straight, and I can't wait to see how God uses you for good in this world. Cannon, you are an incredible hugger and such a joy. Don't ever lose the love you have for others. What a joy it is to be your father, Cannon.

Jess.

I owe everything to Jesus and the rest to you. Being friends at sixteen and seventeen, I would have laughed with happiness and overwhelming joy if you had told me this would be our life. Thank you for your friendship, your love, your hard words, your encouragement, and for never letting me settle. Thank you for always saying yes to the dreams . . . and for your support when they don't always work out. You are so gracious and kind. You are a true visible testimony to the grace of God. I certainly didn't earn or deserve our relationship and intimacy . . . but it's what he's extended to me through you. Visible grace you are.

I never would have gotten to the place of writing this book if it hadn't been for you. I wanted to give up—but you wouldn't let me. And I'm so glad you didn't. I love you so much.

Discussion
Guide

Introduction

1. Nick opens the book with a depiction of his own "I give up" moment. When have you had a moment like that in your own life? What were the circumstances that brought you there?

2. "Exhausted," "defeated," "dry," "ineffective." These are all words Nick uses to describe how this season felt. What other adjectives would you use to describe how you feel in those seasons?

3. How does Nick define *resistance*? What's an example of resistance you are experiencing now or have experienced in the past?

4. It's important to understand present resistance won't be a future reality. Picture yourself one, three, or even five years from now. How do you feel? How are you exercising persistence?

Chapter 1: A Time to Quit

1. When we encounter resistance, how do we know when to keep going? What are some signs of a situation that tell us to walk away?

2. Nick encourages us to use discernment in our decision-making. Are there areas of your life where you might need a "pause" or a "pivot" in order to persist?

Chapter 2: Embracing Storms

1. Nick lives in a geographic region that experiences beautiful weather but also severe tropical storms. What do you love about where you live? What are its risks/dangers? How do you prepare for the latter and know how to weather them?

2. What would be different in our lives and in our relationships with God if we *expected* resistance, instead of being continually surprised by it?

3. How would you describe the differences between pure joy and false joy?

4. "Every good and worthwhile endeavor is met with resistance." Why is this?

Chapter 3: Surrounded by a Cloud

1. In order to remind us that resistance is absolutely
    normal, Nick shares stories of heroes of the faith who
    faced and overcame resistance with God's help. Which
    of these is most meaningful to you and why? What
    other such stories from the Bible, from literature, or
    from history inspire you?

2. Do you see yourself in God's greater story? If these
    heroes have overcome resistance, do you believe you
    can as well?

3. "God isn't a microwave. God isn't an Instant Pot. God is
    like a _____." How does Nick finish this sentence
    and why? Do you agree with his analogy? Why or why
    not?

Chapter 4: Manna in the Cushions:
When Doubt Comes Knocking

1. Nick describes doubt as speaking through a
   megaphone. What doubts have you experienced in
   your own life, and what makes it difficult to dispel
   them? Not all internal voices are good, right, and true.
   How can you differentiate between the voice of the
   Father and the voice of doubt?

2. What is the difference between expectations and
   expectancy?

3. Do you have an example of a time when manna has showed up in your life?

4. Think of a doubt you're currently facing. How would you answer Nick's three questions:

   Is what I'm choosing to believe distracting?
   Is what I'm believing isolating?
   Is what I'm believing limiting?

5. If the answer to these questions is yes, what might that tell you about the nature of the doubt?

Chapter 5: A Thousand Deaths:
When Hardship Hits

1. What is Nick referring to when he describes
    experiencing "a thousand little deaths?" Can you relate
    to this feeling?

2. What does Nick say is our first priority when
    persevering through hardship? Why can doing so feel
    so difficult and counterintuitive? What examples does
    the Bible give of why God wants us to do so?

3. What is, and is not, your responsibility in the face
    of hardship and even tragedy? Are there current
    responsibilities you are carrying that aren't yours to
    carry?

Chapter 6: Searching for Presence:
When God Seems Silent

1. "Nothing lights up a person quite like knowing they've been seen." Who is a person who really sees you, or what is a time when you have felt truly seen? What makes this so meaningful?

2. Nick describes one of his favorite things about Jesus. What is one of your favorite things about him?

3. In considering your calling, Nick asks: What did God last ask you to do? Where did he last ask you to do it? What parts of the Bible resonated with you the most in the past? How would you answer these questions?

Chapter 7: A Parade of People:
When Rejection Is Our Only Friend

1. When was an early or a significant time you "made the unwelcome acquaintance of rejection?"

2. What are some healthy, and unhealthy, ways to deal with rejection?

3. How would you describe the relationship between forgiveness and persistence?

4. Does forgiveness always have to look the same? How so or why not?

Chapter 8: Awakened by Attack:
When Satan Goes on the Offensive

1. Satan "doesn't always cause our hardships," says Nick, "but he definitely capitalizes on them." Do you believe this is true? Why or why not?

2. How does Jesus serve as a model for what to do during spiritual attack?

3. In Ephesians 6, Paul gives us a blueprint of sorts for fighting back during spiritual attack. Do you find yourself giving in to spiritual attack or fighting back?

Chapter 9: The Fog Rolls In:
When Depression Blocks the Sun

1. What is the benefit to identifying and naming
    something in your life like depression, isolation, or
    distance from God?

2. Nick describes depression as "a voice from within that
    sounds like God but it is furthest from the heart of your
    Father." How can you discern the true voice from the
    false ones?

3. What is the difference between taking a moment to withdraw, and becoming isolated and alone?

4. Finish Nick's sentences: "A gentle whisper makes me want to _____ ____. A harsh voice makes me want to _____ _____." How do you see this play out in human relationships? In Scripture?

Chapter 10: The Slow Cooker of Our Souls:
When God Says Wait

1. What does learning to "wait well" look like?

2. Do you believe the wait will ultimately be worth it? How
    so or why not?

3. What are some healthy activities and habits that will
    allow you to be active while you wait?

Chapter 11: Grace for the Give-Ups

1. On a normal day do you find yourself operating more out of feelings of guilt or grace? Out of obligation or God-given opportunity?

2. How does grace make the difference when we have already given up on something that we should have persevered in? How does an understanding of grace change how we feel about and see ourselves? Have you genuinely received the grace of God for your past "give-ups"?

3. What does Nick do every time he's tempted to give up on something good? Why does it help?

Chapter 12: Fighting Back

1. What tools in Nick's "persistence toolbox" might work for you? What other ideas do you have for tools you could use? What are other ways you can challenge your mind, body, and soul to discover there's more persistence in you than you realize?

Chapter 13: Dream the Dreams

1. How can dreaming about the future help produce a daily faith?

2. Take a moment to ask yourself if you've buried any God-given dreams. What would it look like to resurrect those dreams?

3. What are some of the dreams on your own heart right now? Be specific. Take some time now to talk to God about them. If you've had a dream that won't be fulfilled on this side of heaven, talk to God about that too.

Chapter 14: The Harvest Ahead

1. Sometimes we get to experience a breakthrough on the other side of hard times and persistence. "Why does God do this?" Nick asks. "Is it because we've finally done enough, we've finally done it right? I don't think it's as much about our goodness as it is about his goodness." What does Nick mean by this?

2. What does it mean to you that our tears aren't wasted?

3. What have you learned in this book to encourage yourself and others not to give up? What might we lose if we do? How might it help us to persist through hard times if we know and believe that resurrection and restoration are coming on the other side?

4. Who in your life might benefit from receiving a copy of this book?

Notes

CHAPTER 1: A TIME TO QUIT

1. "The Gambler," written and performed by Kenny Rogers, track 1 on compact disc *The Gambler*, Capital Records, Nashville, Tennessee, released 1978.

2. "Obey God and leave all the consequences to him" is a phrase Charles Stanley coined that has always stuck with me. See, for example, Charles Stanley, "Obey God and Leave the Consequences to Him," Dallas Theological Seminary, video, 36:01, accessed March 10, 2023, https://www.youtube.com /watch?v=kLuUvTyE8i8.

CHAPTER 3: SURROUNDED BY A CLOUD

1. See 2 Samuel 7:11-16, where God promises David a descendant whose Kingdom will never end.

CHAPTER 6: SEARCHING FOR PRESENCE

1. "God with us" (see Matthew 1:23).

CHAPTER 12: FIGHTING BACK

1. Eugene H. Peterson, *A Long Obedience in the Same Direction: Discipleship in an Instant Society* (Downers Grove, IL: IVP, 1980).

2. *Abide in Christ* and *With Christ in the School of Prayer* are my favorites.

3. John Eldredge, *Get Your Life Back: Everyday Practices for a World Gone Mad* (Nashville, TN: Nelson, 2020), 25.

About the Author

NICK CONNOLLY is the founding and lead pastor of Bright City Church, a ten-year-old faith community located in the heart of downtown Charleston, South Carolina. Not only is Nick passionate about church, he and his wife, Jess, have started multiple small businesses and love how business can be used for the Kingdom. Nick and Jess live in Charleston with their four kids: Elias, Glory, Benja, and Cannon.

don't give up